Merry·go·round the·Bible

Merry-Go-Round is published by
Scripture Union
Resources For Ministry Unit
PO Box 77, Lidcombe
NSW 2141 Australia.

© 1996 Scripture Union Australia
Edited by John Tigwell

Scripture text from the Contemporary English Version
© American Bible Society 1991, 1995. Used by permission.

National Library of Australia
ISBN 0 949720 61 5

Design & cover by Stephen Stanley & Ivan Smith
Desk Top Publishing by Communique Graphics, Surrey Hills
Printed by New Litho, Surrey Hills

Table of Contents

Page

Introduction

1	Jesus coming soon	Advent 1	1
2	Getting ready for Christmas	Advent 2	4
3	Jesus is born	Christmas 1	8
4	Happy New Year	New Year	11
5	The light keeps shining	Christmas 2	15
6	God the Creator	Summer	18
7	Sing a joyful song	A holiday in summer	22
8	Trust God	An exciting week	25
9	Moses		29
10	Isaiah		32
11	David		36
12	Life as it should be	Lent 1	39
13	Obedience	Lent 2	43
14	Jesus dies	Easter 1	46
15	Jesus is risen	Easter 2	50
16	Stories Jesus told	Part 1	53
17	And the Spirit came	Pentecost	57
18	You give hope	Spring	60
19	When sad things happen		64
20	Abraham		67
21	God bless you	When visitors come	71
22	Joshua		74
23	Samuel		78
24	A wonderful harvest	Autumn	81
25	Each day that we live	A week with a birthday	85
26	Daniel		88
27	Bible heroes – Josiah		92
28	Good news	A holiday in winter	95
29	Stories Jesus told 2		99
30	A dangerous time	Winter	102

Introduction

"I know we ought to but somehow it never happens."

This is often the comment of very sincere parents who have just found the concept of family prayers too hard. There is a lot of material about, but it often requires creativity, glue, pens, paper and time – too daunting a task over a family meal.

Merry-Go-Round has been designed to take about three minutes. It requires no preparation, just the will to get everyone together for a few moments. It makes no assumptions, just that there will be at least one adult available and one child. The text of the Bible from the Contemporary English Version is included in the book, followed by a short comment and a prayer in larger type that can be read by a child.

Merry-Go-Round has 30 weeks' material. This allows for repetition of favourite themes and the fact that some weeks will just be a disaster! Each week has five readings, one for each week day. There is one weekend reading to use at the beginning of the week at a convenient time. Read the introduction to the week then the weekend reading. You could split this into two days if you want to keep up continuity. The book is arranged to follow the church year but can be started anywhere and themes picked out that are suitable for your family.

John Tigwell

Contributors

John Tigwell   Harry Cotter
Jennifer Reay   Robyn Attwood
Pam Griffin

Help! What next?

Well, you have bought a copy of **Merry-Go-Round** or someone has given you a copy – now what? You've never tried family prayers before – where do you start?

First of all, **be enthusiastic**. You don't need a solemn face and a deep voice for family prayers. "Hey kids, we've found this awesome new book to look at all together!" "It's great the way Sally is reading so well now. We've got this great idea for all of us to have a go at reading."

Set a time each day when everyone is present most of the time. The morning at breakfast is a good time but often one or other of the family has to dash out, so the evening meal might be better. Another possibility is just before the younger members' bed time. Be realistic. To set a time which is just before a favourite TV show will hardly encourage concentration, but the end of a TV show with the TV off for a little while might be a good idea. Sometimes we forget the on switch is also the off switch! Before you begin, make sure everyone is ready – food finished, little ones to the toilet and perhaps the phone off the hook or the answer phone on. It's only for a few minutes so people can try again.

You will find a routine sets in; when that is done add variety. Take breakfast into the garden on a fine morning and have a picnic, then do family prayers.

continued overpage ...

Involve the children – good readers could manage any part of the day's reading and most young readers can manage the prayer. At other times during the day, talk about what you read, ask questions, point out truths and encourage the whole family to make talking about God as natural as talking about the weather.

It sounds like a cop out. Surely family prayers should be an event with plenty of time to read and pray. Well, yes, that would be great but we have to be realistic. Life in the average household with young children can be very hectic.

Therefore **Merry-Go-Round** allows families to set realistic goals that can be achieved. It allows for a God-centred oasis in the day and sets a pattern that can be developed as families grow and change. Our prayer is that **Merry-Go-Round** will be a valuable addition to the Scripture Union range of Bible reading guides suitable for every age.

Jesus is coming soon

Advent 1

*A*dvent is all about getting ready. God sent a person to get things ready for Jesus. We will be reading about him this week. His name was John. He was a very special person with a very special job. God chose John to help prepare people to listen to Jesus. He sent him to tell people to say sorry for the way they had disobeyed God. He was so good at doing this that thousands of people came out of the cities and villages to listen to him. When they had said sorry for making God disappointed, John baptised them in the river. This was a special sign to show that people really meant what they said.

As we come up to the Christmas season, let's get our hearts ready for Jesus.

WE. John's message

 You, my son, will be called a prophet of God in heaven above. You will go ahead of the Lord to get everything ready for him. You will tell his people that they can be saved when their sins are forgiven. God's love and kindness will shine upon us like the sun that rises in the sky. On us who live in the dark shadow of death, this light will shine to guide us into a life of peace.

Luke 1:76-79

'Quick, tidy up your room. Scrub the toilet, she'll be here soon!' Is that what happens at our place when a visitor is coming? God wanted someone to get things ready for Jesus. Zechariah and Elizabeth's little baby John was the person God chose. When John grew up, he didn't tell people to tidy their homes or clean their bodies. He told them to prepare their lives for Jesus, to get their minds and hearts ready to learn about him and love him. How can we get ready for Jesus?

This weekend, why don't all of us do one special thing to get ready for Christmas. We could make a present, tidy a cupboard or write some cards. This will remind us that getting ready for Jesus is very important.

1 To let you know the truth

Many people have tried to tell the story of what God has done among us. They wrote what we had been told by the ones who were there in the beginning and saw what happened. So I made a careful study of everything and then decided to write and tell you exactly what took place. Honourable Theophilus, I have done this to let you know the truth about what you have heard.

Luke 1:1-4

'Right', said the detective, 'Tell me exactly what you saw.' It is dangerous but exciting to witness a crime. You are called an eyewitness. Your information may help the police catch a robber, or someone worse! Luke, whose book is in the Bible, didn't see Jesus when Jesus lived on earth, but he took notice of those who did – the eyewitnesses. They were the people who had been with Jesus. Some of them wrote down what they'd seen and heard. Others told people who told more people and so on. So Luke got his information from eyewitnesses. We can be sure Luke's information is true, not a fairytale or a lie, but the truth about Jesus.

Dear God, we thank you that hundreds of years ago people like Luke wrote down the facts about Jesus so that we could know about him.

2 John's parents

When Herod was king of Judea, there was a priest by the name of Zechariah from the priestly group of Abijah. His wife Elizabeth was from the family of Aaron. Both of them were good people and pleased the Lord God by obeying all that he had commanded. But they had no children. Elizabeth couldn't have any and both Zechariah and Elizabeth were already old.

Luke 1:5-7

What sort of a person are you? What do other people think about you? People thought Zechariah and Elizabeth were good people. They spent their lives doing what God wanted – loving him and loving others. Yet they had a great sadness – they really wanted a child but it seemed as if it would never happen. Sometimes when we don't get what we want we mope around feeling sorry for ourselves. We stop doing some of our jobs or seeing friends because all we can think about is our very big problem and disappointment. But Zechariah and Elizabeth kept on being faithful, doing God's work day after day, week after week, month after month, year after year. What a great example to us.

Dear God, help us to be good people, loving and faithful to you and others. Thank you too for all the good people that we know, because they make our lives so much better.

3 Answered prayer

4 Struck dumb

All at once an angel from the Lord appeared to Zechariah at the right side of the altar. Zechariah was confused and afraid when he saw the angel. But the angel told him, "Don't be afraid, Zechariah! God has heard your prayers. Your wife Elizabeth will have a son, and you must name him John. His birth will make you very happy, and many people will be glad."

Luke 1:11-14

Zechariah said to the angel, "How will I know this is going to happen? My wife and I are both very old." The angel answered, " I am Gabriel, God's servant, and I was sent to tell you this good news. You haven't believed what I've said. So you won't be able to say a thing until all this happens. But everything will take place when it is supposed to."

Luke 1:18-20

What's the best news you've had lately? Gabriel, God's good news angel, brought the happiest news to Zechariah and Elizabeth. They were old and had been praying for a child for a long time. Sometimes we pray for something and when we don't get an answer straight away, we give up. God tells us to keep on praying. He always listens to our prayers and we can be sure that he will answer in the right way, at the right time, for the right purposes. Elizabeth's baby would be born at exactly the right time so that he could do the job God had planned for him. So let's keep on praying and keep on looking for God's answers.

Sometimes we want to believe something but it seems too good to be true! The funny thing is that when God gives something it is good because he is true. God isn't a liar. He doesn't give a promise such as 'I will be with you always', and then say 'I was only teasing. I won't do that at all.' So when Zechariah wasn't sure about the angel's message, it was very serious. He lost the ability to speak. Imagine if we couldn't speak for months. Does someone in our family think that's a great idea? The point is, do we believe what we read in the Bible – all those things God said about caring for us, helping us and being with us always? Do we believe them? We should.

Dear God, we thank you for the prayers you have already answered. Help us to ask for things for the right reasons. Help us to keep on praying even though nothing seems to be happening.

Lord, we know many things that you have said. You love us, you are with us and you will help us. It seems hard to believe sometimes. Help us to believe what you say and trust you always.

5 His name is John

Getting ready for Christmas 2

When Elizabeth's son was born, her neighbours and relatives heard how kind the Lord had been to her, and they too were glad ... Zechariah asked for a writing tablet. Then he wrote, "His name is John." Everyone was amazed. Straight away, Zechariah started speaking and praising God.

Luke 1:57 and 63-64

Some people are named after their parents or grandparents. Who in our family is named after someone? Everyone expected Elizabeth's baby to be called after his dad. But that was not to be. God gave him a name. God wanted everyone to know how important this baby was. When John grew up he would do a special job. So when we think of baby John we remember a special person, a special job, a special name. In those days, the name John meant 'The Lord has shown favour'. God gave Zechariah and Elizabeth the best favour they could have imagined. Has anyone done you a favour lately? When we start to count up the ways God has shown favour to us, we could keep on counting for ever and ever. Think of one way God has shown favour to us lately.

Dear Lord, every day you show favour to us. Thank you for giving us life. Thank you for our family and friends. Like old Zechariah, we praise you for all the good things you do.

Advent 2

John was a fisherman who became a follower of Jesus. When he was an old man he wrote down many things he knew about Jesus in a book called 'Revelation', the very last book in the Bible.

John was sent into exile away from his family and friends. He was exiled because he taught people about Jesus. Cut off from his friends, he had lots of time to pray. God gave him a special vision to encourage him and every other Christian who is punished for following Jesus.

Parts of 'Revelation' can be quite difficult to understand but it helps us see how incredible Jesus is and how wonderful our future will be with him.

Coming soon

 Looking forward

 Then I was told, "These words are true and can be trusted. The Lord God controls the spirits of his prophets, and he is the one who sent his angel to show his servants what must happen straight away. Remember, I am coming soon! God will bless everyone who pays attention to the message of this book."

Revelation 22:6-7

Although the book of Revelation is sometimes hard to understand, one thing is plain. Jesus said he is coming back. When will it be? He says it will be soon so we must make sure we are ready. When a sergeant in the army tells his soldiers to pay attention, they immediately stand straight and still, waiting for the next instruction. Jesus tells us to pay attention. Are we paying attention to God's book? It has so many wonderful instructions for us and one of the best is that Jesus is coming soon.

This weekend we could play a game where everyone needs to pay attention, such as 'Simon Says' or 'Statues'.

 "God's home is now with his people. He will live with them, and they will be his own. Yes, God will make his home among his people. He will wipe all tears from their eyes and there will be no more death, suffering, crying or pain. These things of the past are gone forever."

Revelation 21:3b-4

Has anyone ever called you a cry baby? It's embarrassing isn't it? But when you think of it, there is no one who has never ever cried. We all do it. Jesus cried when his friend died. Some of us only cry when no one's looking and that's fine, God understands. But the Bible has great news. When Jesus comes again and we go to heaven, there will be no more crying because there will be nothing sad, painful or frightening to make us cry. Some people go through a lot of suffering – bad things happen to them or the people they love. Some children suffer because they haven't got enough to eat. Others are born with a body that doesn't work properly. We can look forward to that time when all the sad things will be gone for ever.

 Lord God, please help all those today who are crying through sadness, sickness and bad things. Thank you that we can look forward to that time when there will be no more crying.

2 I will be their God

 # 3 God's glory

 "I am making everything new. Write down what I have said. My words are true and can be trusted. Everything is finished! I am Alpha and Omega, the beginning and the end. I will freely give water from the life-giving fountain to everyone who is thirsty. All who win the victory will be given these blessings. I will be their God, and they will be my people."

Revelation 21:5b-7

In the ancient Greek alphabet, the first letter is Alpha and the last is Omega. God is our Alpha and Omega. He is with us at our beginning when we're born and he will be with us at the end. But with God there will never really be an end, because after this life we can live forever with him. He is our God right now but there are some things we don't understand about him. In heaven we will know everything. We don't have to wait for heaven to live as God's people. We can do it now although we won't do it perfectly. We can look forward to the time when we will live with him perfectly in heaven. Then we will know for sure, without a doubt or question, that he is our God.

 We are so glad that you are our God. Thank you that we can live with you in heaven forever. Help us to show others that we are also your people here on earth.

 I didn't see a temple there. The Lord God All-Powerful and the Lamb were its temple. And the city didn't need the sun or the moon. The glory of God was shining on it, and the Lamb was its light.

Revelation 21:22-23

Imagine what life would be like if we had no light. Brushing our teeth would be messy and so would baking a cake. Just now, think of three or four things that give light. Here are some ideas – the sun, a torch, a sparkler. The Bible writer tells us something else that gives light – the glory of God. God's glory will light up heaven. There will be no need for electricity or solar energy. But what is God's glory? Glory is one of those words we use when something is absolutely fantastically terrific and we can hardly describe it. God is far more intelligent, wonderful, loving, wise than we can ever imagine. That's another good reason we can look forward to being with him in heaven. No one will look after us as well as he.

 Father, you are absolutely wonderful. Fantastic. Terrific. You are full of glory. Help us to understand you and tell others how great you are.

Everyone welcome

 Nations will walk by the light of that city, and kings will bring their riches there. Its gates are always open during the day, and night never comes. The glorious treasures of nations will be brought into the city. ... Only those whose names are written in the Lamb's book of life will be in the city.

Revelation 21:24-26 and 27b

Did you see the opening ceremony of the Olympic Games? It was a wonderful sight – all those people from many nations walking into the stadium. It will be even more wonderful in heaven because people from every nation will be there. Even though God sent Jesus to the country known as Israel, he came for the whole world. All those who love him will be in heaven. God even has our names in a book. Many of us love sport, but most of us will never enter a stadium to represent our country. Only the very best sports people are chosen for that. Thankfully, in heaven all are welcome, not just the very best, the most talented, the richest or the most beautiful, but all the people who love Jesus. That's something to really look forward to.

 Dear Lord Jesus, thank you that in heaven all of us can be with you, no matter where we are from or what our abilities may be.

The fruit of the tree of life

 The angel showed me a river that was crystal clear and its waters gave life. The river came from the throne where God and the Lamb were seated. Then it flowed down the middle of the city's main street. On each side of the river are trees that grow a different kind of fruit each month of the year. The fruit gives life, and the leaves are used as medicine to heal the nations.

Revelation 22:1-2

What will heaven look like? We all imagine it differently. That's fine, God hasn't told us everything about it. But the book of Revelation gives hints. It mentions a river with fruit trees on either side. It sounds beautiful and refreshing. When Adam and Eve were in the garden of Eden there was a tree in the middle called the tree of life. Did you know they had to leave that perfect, safe place because they disobeyed God? How wonderful that heaven will be perfect and safe. There will once again be fruit trees with fruit that will give us life. When you think of all the exciting, wonderful things we sometimes do in our lives here, it makes us think WOW! Life in heaven will be absolutely great!

 Father God, thank you that life in heaven will be better than anything we have ever known.

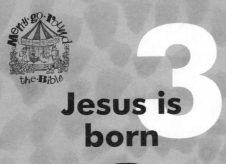

Jesus is born **3**

Christmas 1

*I*t's nearly Christmas! All around the world millions of people are going to church services and worshipping God. Carols are being sung, children are dressing up as shepherds and wise men and angels. It is a time to celebrate and a time to remember. This week we will read about when Jesus was born. It begins with an ordinary girl in Nazareth and ends with a magnificent heavenly choir of angels. At Christmas, earth and heaven, people and God are brought together. That's why we have special celebrations. It's Jesus' birthday – the most wonderful birthday that ever was.

WE. Peace on earth

Suddenly many other angels came down from heaven and joined in praising God. They said, "Praise God in heaven! Peace on earth to everyone who pleases God." After the angels had left and gone back to heaven, the shepherds said to each other, "Let's go to Bethlehem and see what the Lord has told us about." They hurried off and found Mary and Joseph, and they saw the baby lying on a bed of hay.

Luke 2:13-16

Did anyone sing when you were born? When God's son was born there was a choir of angels. They gave a free concert to a bunch of startled shepherds singing about peace on earth. The birth of Jesus and peace on earth go together. Peace is the opposite of fighting and arguing. When we live our own way instead of God's, it's as if we are his enemies fighting against him. Jesus came so we could be God's friends and not his enemies. Peace on earth – what a great thing to remember this Christmas!

We could make a family peace flag on a large piece of paper. This can remind us to try to live peacefully with each other. Most of all it can help us remember the peace we can have with God.

Mary the mother of Jesus

One month later God sent the angel Gabriel to the town of Nazareth in Galilee with a message for a virgin named Mary. She was engaged to Joseph from the family of King David. The angel greeted Mary and said, "You are truly blessed! The Lord is with you." ... Then the angel told Mary, "Don't be afraid! God is pleased with you, and you will have a son. His name will be Jesus."

Luke 1:26-28 and 30-31

What plans have we made that didn't turn out the way we expected? Mary's plans didn't turn out as she expected. She was engaged, planning her marriage and her life with Joseph. She never dreamed things would work out the way they did. What do you imagine Mary was doing when the angel appeared? Sweeping the floor? Baking bread? No one knows, but when Gabriel (God's good news angel) appeared, she was frightened. He told her she would have a baby, God's son. Many artists have painted beautiful pictures of Mary. Of course we don't know what she really looked like, but from what the Bible tells us she must have been a person with a beautiful gentle heart, just right for the mother of Jesus.

Lord, Mary must have been so special because you chose her to look after your son. Thank you Lord for every mother.

Mary's song

Mary said, "With all my heart I praise the Lord, and I am glad because of God my Saviour. God cares for me, his humble servant. From now on, all people will say God has blessed me. God All-Powerful has done great things for me, and his name is holy. He always shows mercy to everyone who worships him."

Luke 1:46-50

This song shows us the sort of person Mary was. She had just been chosen for a most important job, to be the mother of Jesus. Sometimes when people are chosen for important things they show off and want others to see how great they are. Not Mary. She called herself God's 'humble servant'. That's what she was before the angel came and that's what she intended to be afterwards. A wonderful thing about God is that he often chooses people who aren't very important to do his important work. The Bible is full of examples, such as Gideon, a farmer who won a great battle; Ruth, a poor girl who became the grandmother of Israel's greatest king; and now Mary. These people were God's humble servants and he blessed them.

Dear God, help us to be your humble servants too. Thank you for all the ways you have blessed us.

The journey to Bethlehem

 # Jesus is born

 About that time Emperor Augustus gave orders for the names of all the people to be listed in record books... Everyone had to go to their own home town to be listed. So Joseph had to leave Nazareth in Galilee and go to Bethlehem in Judea. Long ago Bethlehem had been King David's home town, and Joseph went there because he was from David's family.

Luke 2:1 and 3-4

Some journeys are exciting, for example going on a holiday or travelling to see friends. But some journeys are different – we'd rather stay home. Mary and Joseph had to make a journey to Bethlehem. This didn't come at a good time. Mary was pregnant and knew she would soon have her baby. Many people think she rode on a donkey. We don't really know. Perhaps Mary would have preferred to stay in Nazareth so she could have the baby near her family. But God knew what he was doing. Hundreds of years before, God's messengers had said the Saviour would be born in Bethlehem, not an important place but the place God chose for his son's birth. God often surprises us with his plans. Are we ready to fit in with God's plans even though they make us feel uncomfortable?

 Father God, help us to do what is right so that we show our love for you.

 Mary was engaged to Joseph and travelled with him to Bethlehem. She was soon going to have a baby, and while they were there, she gave birth to her firstborn son. She dressed him in baby clothes and laid him on a bed of hay, because there was no room for them in the inn.

Luke 2:5-7

Many artists have done paintings of the night Jesus was born. You can see some in library books. Some paintings show people dressed in beautiful clothes and around people's faces is a shining light. It looks so beautiful and peaceful. Yet it may have been different. Mary and Joseph couldn't even find one room in a hotel, so Jesus was born in a place where animals were kept. Can you imagine a baby having to sleep in a dog's kennel or a cat's basket? The first bed for baby Jesus was an animal's wooden feed box full of hay. The people in Bethlehem didn't think Mary or Joseph were very important, otherwise they would have helped them find a better place to stay. They didn't realise that the baby Mary fed and rocked to sleep was the Saviour of the world.

 Dear God, when Jesus was born many people didn't think he was important. We know he is our Saviour. May we worship him always.

The good news

That night in the fields near Bethlehem some shepherds were guarding their sheep. All at once an angel came down to them from the Lord, and the brightness of the Lord's glory flashed around them. The shepherds were frightened. But the angel said, "Don't be afraid! I have good news for you, which will make everyone happy. This very day in King David's home town a Saviour was born for you. He is Christ the Lord."

Luke 2:8-11

Have you ever been in the spotlight? Was it a real light on a stage or were you the centre of attention? Something like that happened to the shepherds. One minute they were minding their sheep, next they were standing in the flashing spotlight of God's glory! Scary stuff! No wonder they were afraid. The light came with angels who brought the best news ever – for them and for us. Jesus our Saviour was born. God first gave this important news to unimportant shepherds who didn't think they were important at all. Jesus came to be their saviour and ours. That really is good news.

We thank you God, for the best news ever that tells us that Jesus was born. Thank you for sending him for everyone, even for shepherds and children.

Happy New Year 4

New Year

January is a great time to make decisions for the whole year. This week the readings are about Joshua. Joshua helped the Israelites to make decisions they could keep for the whole of their lives. Let's see what they were. We will find they are decisions we can make too.

The problem with New Year resolutions is that they are very hard to keep. However, if we make wise decisions, God will give us the strength to keep our resolution. He certainly helped Joshua keep his promises.

Worship and obey

 # Be faithful

Not long afterwards, the Lord's servant Joshua died at the age of 110. The Israelites buried him in his own land at Timnath-Serah, north of Mount Gaash in the hill country of Ephraim. As long as Joshua lived, Israel worshipped and obeyed the Lord. There were other leaders old enough to remember everything that the Lord had done for Israel. And for as long as these men lived, Israel continued to worship and obey the Lord.

Joshua 24:29-31

What a great leader was Joshua! He was a great army commander but that's not all. He was great because he helped people to love God. When Joshua was younger, he was sent as a spy to check out the land of Canaan. Eleven other spies went too. Ten came back and said, 'It's very scary. We can't go and live there.' But Joshua and his friend Caleb said, 'Yes, it's very scary but we can go and live there because God will be with us.' Joshua and Caleb were proved to be right. As Joshua became older he kept on trusting God. People admired Joshua and wanted to worship and obey God just as he did.

This weekend we could make a list of people who have helped us to worship and obey God. You might like to write them a thank you note.

Be sure that you carefully obey everything written in 'The Book of the Law' of Moses and do exactly what it says. Don't have anything to do with the nations that live around you. Don't worship their gods or pray to their idols or make promises in the names of their gods. Be as faithful to the Lord as you have always been.

Joshua 23:6-8

A faithful friend will always be your friend no matter what. God is a faithful friend to those who trust him. Have you ever thought, 'I know God is faithful to me but am I faithful to God?' The great leader Joshua reminded the Israelites who were living among people who worshipped pretend gods that they should not copy their neighbours. Sometimes we copy others at work or school so they will be our friends. But if others act as if they don't love God, will we be faithful to him? Or will we go along with the others? God understands how hard it is for us to be different. As this year begins, let's pray that we will be strong and brave enough to be faithful to God.

 Dear God, you are always faithful to us. May we always be faithful to you.

2 God keeps his promise

3 We will obey the Lord

I will die soon, as everyone must. But deep in your hearts you know that the Lord has kept every promise he ever made to you. Not one of them has been broken.

Joshua 23:14

When Joshua said that God keeps promises he knew what he was talking about. God kept his promises to Joshua. When Joshua became the leader of his people, God said, 'I will always be with you and help you ... no one will ever be able to defeat you' (Joshua 1:5). Over the years God kept that promise. God promised his people they would have a land of their own and Joshua was actually with them when this happened. Although God's promises in the Bible were given to people long ago, some of them are for us today. God is a promise keeper not a promise breaker. Sometimes we may wonder if God is keeping his promises but if we wait patiently we will see that he always does.

Dear God, help us always to trust you and remember that you always keep your promises.

Then Joshua told the people: "Worship the Lord, obey him, and always be faithful. Get rid of the idols your ancestors worshipped when they lived on the other side of the Euphrates River and in Egypt. But if you don't want to worship the Lord, then choose right now! Will you worship the same idols your ancestors did? Or since you're living in the land that once belonged to the Amorites, maybe you'll worship their gods. I won't. My family and I are going to worship and obey the Lord."

Joshua 24:14-15

Decisions, decisions. There are so many we have to make. The most important we can make this year is 'Are we going to worship and obey God?' It's as simple as that. Obeying God means living his way which means loving others. Loving others shows in the decisions we make. So the jobs we do, the games we play, the way we treat others, are all tied in with obeying God. We can make this decision for ourselves, but we can make it with our families too, as Joshua did. The important thing is not how many people are in our family or how much money we've got or what sort of place we live in. More important is whether our family decides this year to worship and obey God.

God our Father, as this year begins help us as a family to worship and obey you.

Set free

The people answered, "We could never worship other gods or stop worshipping the Lord. The Lord is our God. We were slaves in Egypt as our ancestors had been, but we saw the Lord work miracles to set our people free and to bring us out of Egypt. Even though other nations were all around us, the Lord protected us wherever we went."

Joshua 24:16-17

Do you know the game 'Stuck in the Mud', where someone is trapped and another person has to free them? It's a great feeling when someone frees you. Imagine how great the Israelites felt when God set them free from being slaves in Egypt. They had been treated cruelly for years. You may know the story. It has Pharaoh, plagues, an angel and a special meal called the Passover. In a way God sets us all free. No Pharaoh is making us his slaves. There are other things from which we need to be set free – sin that leads to our own selfishness and the tricks of God's enemy Satan. It wasn't easy for God to set us free. It meant he had to send his son to die for us. So this year, let's live as God's grateful free people.

Dear God, this year we want to thank you for setting us free. We are free to love you and love others.

Obey the Lord

Joshua said, "The Lord is fearsome; he is the one true God, and I don't think you are able to worship and obey him in the ways he demands. You would have to be completely faithful, and if you sin or rebel, he won't let you get away with it. If you turn your backs on the Lord and worship the gods of other nations, the Lord will turn against you. He will make terrible things happen to you and wipe you out, even though he had been good to you before." But the people shouted, "We won't worship any other gods. We will worship and obey only the Lord!"

Joshua 24:19-21

Who remembers the first words you ever spoke? Was it 'Mamma', 'Dadda' or 'more'? Maybe it was 'No!' Many babies learn to say no loudly and clearly whenever they don't want to do what they are told. If God tells us to do something he wants us to say 'Yes'. That's what obeying God is all about – saying yes to God's commands. When you think of it, God's commands are all very good – things like love him, love others, treat others in the way you want them to treat you. Like the people in Joshua's day, we have to choose whether we will obey God or not. This new year is a good time to say, 'Yes God, we will obey you.'

Help us, Lord, to say yes to your commands.

The light keeps shining

Christmas 2

Now that we've remembered the story of Jesus being born, we can think about who Jesus really is. We know he came as a baby, but why did he come? How great is he? What must we do? The readings we have this week can help us answer these questions.

They were written by John, a special follower of Jesus. John was a very deep thinker. He didn't just write down stories about Jesus, he wrote down special things he heard Jesus say. Because he was getting older, he was able to share the wise things he had discovered about Jesus over the years.

 This is the one

John spoke about him and shouted, "This is the one I told you would come! He is greater than I am, because he was alive before I was born." Because of all that the Son is, we have been given one blessing after another. The Law was given by Moses, but Jesus Christ brought us undeserved kindness and truth. No one has ever seen God. The only Son, who is truly God and is closest to the Father, has shown us what God is like.

John 1:15-18

You may know the game 'Find the Leader'. 'It' goes out of the room while the others choose a leader. The person comes back. The leader does different actions and the others copy. 'It' has to identify the leader.

John was getting things ready for a leader, God's son, but for a long time he didn't know who it was. One day a man was baptised at the river. The Holy Spirit came down on him in a special beautiful way (John 1:32). Immediately John knew this was God's son. It was Jesus. John excitedly said, 'This is the one'. Although John was born before Jesus, John knew that Jesus was really alive before the world began.

This weekend if there are more than three people, we could play the game 'Find the Leader'.

The light keeps shining

In the beginning was the one who is called the Word. The Word was with God and was truly God. From the very beginning the Word was with God. And with this Word, God created all things. Nothing was made without the Word. Everything that was created received its life from him, and his life gave light to everyone. The light keeps shining in the dark and darkness has never put it out.

John 1:1-5

Have you ever tried to light birthday candles and the match keeps going out? Sometimes it's the wind, or someone sneezes. The candles help us celebrate a happy event so we want them to shine. Jesus is sometimes called the light of the world. In this Bible reading he is called the Word and the Light. It's as if all the evil things are darkness and Jesus, with all his goodness and love, is light. God's enemy, Satan, and even some people, try to fight against Jesus, but in the end they will not win. His goodness and love will always be stronger. Does anyone know the song 'Shine Jesus Shine' by Graham Kendrick? That reminds us that in the middle of the darkness Jesus is there for us.

Jesus, sometimes we think of you as the light that has never gone out, always there for us, always full of goodness and love. Thank you for being the light.

John tells the story

God sent a man named John, who came to tell about the light and to lead all people to have faith. John wasn't that light. He came only to tell about the light.

John 1:6-8

Who'd like to be a news reporter searching out the best stories to write? Or a reporter on TV with a microphone in your hand ready for the cameras. Reporters don't usually write about themselves. They tell true stories about others. When John, the son of Elizabeth and Zechariah, grew up he told people about Jesus. Some people thought that John was the most important person around. 'No!' he said. 'Jesus is! I'm just here to tell you to get things ready for him.' There was nothing more important for John to do than to tell others about Jesus. He spent each day doing that, even when it got him into big trouble. John wanted everyone to know that they could have faith in Jesus, God's son, God's light.

Thank you Father for all the people who tell about Jesus at home, at church, at school and other places. Help us to have faith in Jesus always.

No one listens

God's children

The true light that shines on everyone was coming into the world. The Word was in the world, but no one knew him, though God had made the world with his Word. He came into his own world, but his own nation did not welcome him.

John 1:9-11

Imagine it's your birthday and you've invited lots of people to your party. When they arrive, they ignore you. Many don't seem to know who you are. Those who do know you don't seem to realise or care that it's your party. How would you feel? When God sent Jesus into the world, many people didn't know who he really was. If they had listened carefully to God's messengers they would have known he was God's son. But because they hadn't really listened, they thought Jesus was an ordinary person, the son of a carpenter. When Jesus told them who he was, they didn't believe him and called him a liar. Little did they know that Jesus was there at the very beginning of time designing and creating the entire universe. If we had been there, would we have listened to Jesus or would we too have sent him away?

Jesus, help us not to be like those who sent you away. We know how great and loving you are. Help us to listen when others tell us true things about you.

Yet some people accepted him and put their faith in him. So he gave them the right to be the children of God. They were not God's children by nature or because of any human desires. God himself was the one who made them his children.

John 1:12-13

How many people are there in our family? What's the biggest family you know? There's one family that is far bigger than any we know and it keeps on growing. Anyone can belong to it. We're talking about God's family. When we put our faith in Jesus we become children of God. Another word for a child of God is a Christian. You could ask some other Christians you know when they became God's children. Some will say it happened when they were children or teenagers. Others will say they were grown-ups. Some won't remember when it happened because they can't remember a time when they didn't love Jesus. No matter when it happened, isn't it great that we can be God's children and have him as our loving father?

Dear God, we are so thankful that you sent Jesus so that we could become your children.

5 All the truth of God

The Word became a human being and lived here with us. We saw his true glory, the glory of the only Son of the Father. From him all the kindness and all the truth of God have come down to us.

John 1:14

Has anyone ever said to you, 'You're just like your mum' or, 'You're the spitting image of your father'? Usually they mean we look like the other person, but they may mean we are like them in other ways. Hopefully they are giving us a compliment! When Jesus lived on earth, people began to understand what God was like because Jesus is just like his father. So if we want to know the truth about God we should ask ourselves, 'What do we know about Jesus?' Well, he cared for people, he got angry when people were treated unfairly. He forgave people. He was a friend to the people no one else liked. All these things and more show us what God is like. Jesus showed all the kindness and truth about God.

God our Father, we thank you that Jesus shows us what you are like – loving and kind. Help us to be like Jesus and show your love and kindness to others.

God the Creator 6

Summer

Summer is a great time. We have long holidays and we can laze around in the hea doing very little. If we 'slip slop, slap' with the sun-screen lotion we can have a great time outdoors. Even when it thunderstorms and the rain pours down we know it won't last and the sur will soon be out. The Psalm we ar reading this week is a special son about God who made everything. It's a special praise song to say thank you for the world in which we live.

Look out of the window. What car you see that makes you want to say thank you to God? Trees, birds, your dog or cat – lots of different things. What a great God we have.

WE. God the Creator

  # God's good gifts

I praise you Lord God, with all my heart. You are glorious and majestic, dressed in royal robes and surrounded by light. You spread out the sky like a tent, and you built your home over the mighty ocean. The clouds are your chariot with the wind as its wings.

Psalm 104:1-3

The writer of this song is trying to describe God. That's a very difficult thing to do. As he looks out at the mountain and the sky he imagines God involved in everything. The scientists tell us that the atmosphere, 'the sky', keeps the world's climate even so that all the living things on the planet can survive. What things live in our backyard or in the park? (Lizards? Snails? Flowers? Vegetables?) What happens to them when it gets very hot or very wet? God provides them with ways of surviving. Over the weekend, let's look to see how God's creation reacts as the weather changes. If it's hot we might think nothing is around. But we might get a big surprise if we look.

You provide streams of water in the hills and valleys, so that the donkeys and other wild animals can satisfy their thirst. Birds build their nests nearby and sing in the trees. From your home above you send rain on the hills and water the earth. You let the earth produce grass for cattle, plants for our food, wine to cheer us up, olive oil for our skin, and grain for our health.

Psalm 104:10-15

Rain is vital for life. Rain waters the land, fills the rivers and dams. The grass feeds cattle and sheep and the wild animals. We know that when there is a drought everyone suffers – no crops grow and farmers get no money. Cattle and sheep die as do the wild animals. Dust gets in through every crack and settles on every surface. When there is rain, everything is different and people can be happy. We don't know why there are times of drought and flood and other times are just right. We know that this world isn't perfect and God's good creation has been spoiled. So like the writer of this song we can thank God for his creation. We can also pray for people who suffer because the rains fail.

 Dear God, thank you for the rain that allows crops to grow and animals to flourish. Please send rain to areas where there is drought.

2 God's order

Our Lord, your trees always have water, and so do the cedars you planted in Lebanon. Birds nest in those trees, and storks make their home in the fir trees. Wild goats find a home in the tall mountains, and small animals can hide between the rocks. You created the moon to tell us the seasons. The sun knows when to set, and you made the darkness, so the animals in the forest could come out at night.

Psalm 104:16-20

What a wonderful world we live in. God created it so that it had 'order'. Goats can't live under rocks so they are found in high mountains where they are safe. God even made some animals to see so well they can hunt by night. Can you think of some animals who come out looking for food at night? Isn't it great in the summer when the hot sun sets and the world cools down? Everything takes a rest and enjoys the cool breeze. The sounds change and the night noises start. Chirping crickets, croaking frogs and hooting owls are part of the sounds of night.

What a wonderful God we have who not only made the day but thought of night as well – everything in order.

Dear Heavenly Father, thank you for day and for night. Help us to enjoy them both in different ways.

3 God made so many things

Lions roar as they hunt for the food you provide. But when morning comes, they return to their dens, then we go out to work until the end of the day. Our Lord, by your wisdom you made so many things; the whole earth is covered with your living creatures.

Psalm 104:21-24

Have you been to a zoo or read a book about animals? What's the funniest animal you have seen? What is your favourite animal? Every one has been created for a very special purpose. Why did God make blowflies, do you think? There are so many different creatures in the world and God made each one. God also made all the people. He gave us a very special job to look after his world and to care for it. You probably know about 'caring for the environment'. We do that not just because it makes the place better for us, but because it is God's world – he made it and he cares about it. So by recycling our papers and bottles and using water carefully, we are helping look after God's world. But more than that, when we encourage each other to take care of God's world then things really begin to get right.

Dear God, thank you for your creation. Help us today to do our part in looking after your world.

God looks after his Creation

But what about the ocean so big and wide? It is alive with creatures, large and small. And there are the ships, as well as Leviathan, the monster you created to splash in the sea. All of these depend on you to provide them with food, and you feed each one with your own hand, until they are full.

Psalm 104:25-28

The story writer is thinking about the great oceans. Long ago when this story was written, the oceans were frightening places. No one knew what was on the other side – indeed they thought if you went too far you fell off the edge. But the song writer knew that the little fish and the great big whales were all fed and cared for. So he thought of God providing food for them. After all, no person could feed them, they were way out at sea. God's creation is so wonderful — everything fits together and works perfectly unless we humans spoil it. If we overfish the ocean then there are no more fish. If we dump things in the ocean we poison the water. What a great responsibility we have to take care of all the precious things God made.

Lord God, thank you for the great oceans of the world. Thank you for all the fish you make to live in them. Help us to care for your creation.

Praise the Lord

Our Lord, we pray that your glory will last for ever and that you will be pleased with what you have done. You look at the earth, and it trembles. You touch the mountains, and smoke goes up. As long as I live, I will sing and praise you, the Lord God. I hope my thoughts will please you, because you are the one who makes me glad.

Psalm 104:31-34

Thinking about everything God made makes the song writer very glad. He has enjoyed thinking about the sun and the moon, the rivers and the oceans. He probably smiled to himself as he thought about some of the funny creatures God made. He may have shivered with fright when he saw a volcano spitting out smoke and fire. He remembers an earthquake — the ground shook and it was hard to stand up. It is truly an amazing world and God made it all. Look out of the window and thank God for some of the things you can see he created. Flowers, trees, clouds and wind are all part of his purpose. So the writer ends his song by saying, 'With all my heart I praise you.' That's what we should do as we thank God for his creation.

Praise you heavenly father for your creation. Help us to enjoy it and treat it properly.

Sing a
joyful song

A holiday in Summer

The book of Psalms contains many special songs that were written for times of thanksgiving. Psalms 95 and 96 were probably sung at the New Year Festival when everyone travelled up to Jerusalem to worship in the temple. They gathered to thank God for his creation and for the way he had cared for his people. When we are on holiday we can especially think of God and thank him, not just for his creation, but for all the good things he has done for us personally.

WE Sing a joyful song

Sing joyful songs to the Lord! Praise the mighty rock where we are safe. Come to worship him with thankful hearts and songs of praise. The Lord is the greatest God, king over all other gods. He holds the deepest part of the earth in his hands, and the mountain peaks belong to him. The ocean is the Lord's because he made it, and with his own hands he formed the dry land.

Psalm 95:1-5

What a great Psalm! Can you think of songs about God that you would like to sing if you were in the temple? Perhaps we can each choose our favourite? Who can remember the words so we can all join in? Singing joyful songs is a special way of saying thank you to God. It shows how much we appreciate what he has done for us. The writer of this song knew that wherever he went – the deepest part of the earth or the highest mountain – God was there. That's why he invites everyone to worship God with thankful hearts and songs of praise.

Birds and animals sing joyful songs too. While on holidays let's make a list of all the sounds we hear.

Don't be stubborn

Bow down and worship the Lord our Creator! The Lord is our God and we are his people, the sheep he takes care of in his own pasture. Listen to God's voice today! Don't be stubborn and rebel as your ancestors did at Meribah and Massah out in the desert ... In his anger, God told them, "You people will never enter my place of rest."

Psalm 95:6-8,11

Just like a shepherd cares for his sheep so God cares for us. The sheep know the shepherd's voice and come when he calls. So we are to listen to God's voice. Usually that means reading the Bible and letting God speak to us that way. The writer of this song remembered that when God's special people were wandering in the desert they became very stubborn. They wouldn't listen to God and were very disobedient. In the end, God wouldn't let them go into his promised land. How sad to be stubborn and disobey God. How much better to listen to what he says and obey him. That way he will care for us every day.

Dear Heavenly Father, please help me not to be stubborn and go my own way. Help me to listen to you and obey you.

The Lord has saved us

Sing a new song to the Lord! Everyone on this earth, sing praises to the Lord, sing and praise his name. Day after day announce, "The Lord has saved us!" Tell every nation on earth, "The Lord is wonderful and does marvellous things!"

Psalm 96:1-3

As the people gathered in the temple they became more and more excited. People from far away came for the special festival. The temple was full to overflowing. The singers began to sing this beautiful song. They wanted everyone on earth to know that the Lord is wonderful and does marvellous things. It would have been exciting to be there. Have you ever been in a big crowd praising God? The most important thing the singers wanted to tell the world was 'The Lord had saved us.' When this song was written, it told how God had protected his special people and let them live in peace in their land. Today when we sing it we want to tell everyone that Jesus saves and that everyone can be at peace with God. That is a wonderful song to sing.

Lord Jesus, thank you that we can sing praises to you. Thank you that you saved us.

3 Give honour to the Lord

4 Bring an offering

"The Lord is great and deserves our greatest praise! He is the only God worthy of our worship. Other nations worship idols, but the Lord created the heavens. Give honour and praise to the Lord, whose power and beauty fill his holy temple."

Psalm 96:4-6

Some people worship idols. They carve wood or chip stone to make beautiful statues. Then they bow down and pray expecting these gods to help them in their lives. This may seem strange or silly to us but many people in the world think that such idols are very important. It is their way of searching for God. We should not think we are better than them because we can be silly about idols too. How? It is easy to love our money or our things or our sports or TV or hobbies so much that they become like idols for us. They can become more important to us than worshipping God and learning to be his people. It is easy to forget that all the good things in our lives come from God. He's the one who should come first. Forgetting important things can be a trap.

Dear God, help us always to put you first and worship you as you deserve.

Tell everyone of every nation, "Praise the glorious power of the Lord. He is wonderful! Praise him and bring an offering into his temple. Everyone on earth, now tremble and worship the Lord, majestic and holy."

Psalm 96:7-9

God is wonderful. He has done many great things so we should be very careful to obey and honour him. One way to show how much we love him is by sharing what we have. When this song was written, many people brought part of their crops to the temple to say thank you to God. They were expected to bring one tenth of their crop. God still expects us to share what we have with others. We should give not because we must but because we love God and want to do things that please him. Part of that sharing is giving to help God's work in our local church or through other Christian organisations. When this song was first sung, people always brought the best to God: the first lambs of the season and the ripest fruit. Second best won't do for God.

Dear God, please use the money we give our church to help other people hear about Jesus.

5 The Lord is King

Announce to the nations, "The Lord is King! The world stands firm, never to be shaken, and he will judge its people with fairness." Tell the heavens and the earth to be glad and celebrate! Command the ocean to roar with all of its creatures and the fields to rejoice with all of their crops. Then every tree in the forest will sing joyful songs to the Lord. He is coming to judge all people on earth with fairness and truth.

Psalm 96:10-13

The Lord is King says the writer of this Psalm. If that is so, then everyone can be glad. God is fair and what he says is true. We can trust him as the worshippers in the temple trusted him. Therefore, everyone can celebrate and be glad. Can you imagine every tree in the forest singing? It's a picture of a really great party isn't it? Trees singing, oceans roaring and fields rejoicing. The song writer wants to help us understand how excited people were when they sang praises to God thanking him for his goodness. Even the wind in the trees and breaking waves remind him of how great God is. We can think of God when we are out in the country or by the sea and thank him that he is indeed King.

Thank you Lord for all your creation. Thank you for allowing us to praise you and worship you.

Trust God - an exciting week 8

Some weeks are more exciting than others. Is anything special happening at our house this week? Are we waiting for something new to be delivered or is someone special visiting? In all the busyness it's easy to forget that the most exciting thing of all is that God never stops loving us. The Psalm we are reading this week is actually about David. He wrote many Psalms but not this one. God chose David to be king which meant he had huge responsibilities. Maybe this song was sung during a week of celebration when a new king was chosen. The song's message is clear – don't forget God or trouble will come. In the middle of the celebration song is a wonderful truth, that we can be 'happy all day because of you' (Psalm 89:16).

God is interested in everyone

Our Lord, I will sing of your love for ever. Everyone yet to be born will hear me praise your faithfulness. I will tell them, "God's love can always be trusted, and his faithfulness lasts as long as the heavens."

Psalm 89:1-2

Often in the Bible people start to sing a song when they are excited. Does that happen in our home? Singing songs, clapping and dancing show we are excited. We could learn a special song this week to sing whenever we feel excited. It tells us that Jesus goes on loving us whatever happens:

> Jesus love is very wonderful,
> Jesus love is very wonderful,
> Jesus love is very wonderful,
> Oh wonderful love.
>
> So high you can't get over it,
> So low you can't get under it,
> So wide you can't get round it,
> Oh wonderful love.

© Scripture Union

The music is found in lots of different song books and we can make up our own actions for it if we like.

None who live in the heavens can compare with you. You are the most fearsome of all who live in heaven; all the others fear and greatly honour you. You are Lord God All-Powerful! No one is as loving and faithful as you are. You rule the roaring sea and calm its waves ... The heavens and the earth belong to you. And so does the world with all its people because you created them.

Psalm 89:6-9,11

Have you ever made a model, perhaps with a kit or out of Lego or building blocks? It takes a long time. Sometimes it goes wrong and you have to start again. Imagine making the whole world and everything in it. We wouldn't know where to start. But God did. The most important thing he made was you and me. Sometimes when we get excited we get a bit silly and do silly things. We become selfish and don't treat other people very well. God is never like that. He knows everything there is to know about us. That's why he understands what is best for us. It is great to remember God made us and therefore he loves us.

Loving Heavenly Father, thank you for loving each one of us. Help us today to be loving towards each other because we know that will make you happy.

God strong and mighty

Happy all day

You are strong and mighty! Your kingdom is ruled by justice and fairness with love and faithfulness leading the way.

Psalm 89:13-14

How often do we say 'It's not fair'? Sometimes we really mean 'I'm not getting my own way.' That means we are being selfish. Sometimes things aren't fair – the Bible calls this 'unjust'. Sadly, there is a lot of unfairness in the world. When someone is not treated properly, doesn't get their fair share, or is punished for something they didn't do, it's unfair. Humans treat each other badly and so people become sick or hungry. Some have to leave their homes and become refugees, living far away from their homes. When things are going well, God is happy. Never forget that God also loves those people who are treated unfairly and that makes him very sad. God is strong and mighty. He wants us to choose the right things because we love him.

Dear God, we want to praise you and thank you that you are strong and mighty. Please help those people in the world who are being treated unfairly. Remind us and them of your love. Help us to treat each other fairly so we can all be happy together.

Our Lord, you bless those who join in the festival and walk in the brightness of your presence. We are happy all day because of you, and your saving power brings honour to us.

Psalm 89:15-16

The people singing this song were taking part in a special festival to say thank you to God. They were going to the big temple in Jerusalem. It was full of people singing praises to God. They were in party mood wearing colourful clothes. People were very happy. Can you read why they were happy? Because of God's glorious power which protected and cared for them in the past. When God saved them from their enemies, the other people who lived around them saw that God was really strong and mighty. The same goes for us. When we are happy and treat other people fairly, others know that we love God. Can you remember a time when God helped you? The Bible tells us that God is always the same. He helped the people singing this song to be happy. He loved them and cared for them. That's a good reason for us to be happy as well.

Thank you God for loving us. Please help us to remember you today and to be people who show that we belong in your family.

4 God is kind

5 God chooses

Your own glorious power makes us strong, and because of your kindness, our strength increases. Our Lord and our King, the Holy One of Israel, you are truly our shield.

Psalm 89:17-18

Have you seen pictures of soldiers long ago with swords to attack with and shields to defend themselves? When a soldier was hurt and dropped his shield, other soldiers gathered round him and protected him with their shields. That's what the singers are thinking about in these verses. God is powerful and cares for his people. He is kind to them when they are in trouble. He shields them from their enemies. Everyone feels stronger when we are kind to each other. It means we help each other when we have problems and are pleased for each other when we do well. Doing kind things saves us from getting angry with each other and shields us from doing wrong. God is kind to us, giving us the strength to do right things. When that happens we get stronger.

Dear Lord, thank you for giving us the strength to do right things. Help us today to be kind to each other just as you are kind to us.

In a vision, you once said to your faithful followers: "I have helped a mighty hero. I chose him from my people and made him famous. David, my servant, is the one I chose to be king, and I will always be there to help and strengthen him".

Psalm 89:19-21

God chose David to be king. He was only a teenager when Samuel told him he would be king. God was with him all his life. He became famous as a soldier and a general. His first brave deed was when he fought an enormous enemy soldier called Goliath. He defeated Goliath and all the enemies of God's people. Because God chose David, he helped him. David did some very bad things but he remembered God and was sorry. Then God helped him again. God had chosen him and wanted him to lead his people. He stuck by him. God chooses us to be his followers and he is always there ready to help us. When we do wrong things, if we are truly sorry, he will forgive us and help us. It's great to know that God has big strong arms.

Thank you God for choosing us to be your followers. Thank you for being ready to help us. Help us to say sorry when we let you down.

Bible heroes - Moses

9

W hen have we been on a long trip in a car or plane? Was it for a holiday or did we visit someone? What sort of preparation went on before the journey? In the second book of the Bible called Exodus, we read about a long journey God took with his people, the Israelites. He wanted to take them to a beautiful place where they would be free to live the way he wanted them to live. There they could worship him. Moses is the main character in this book. God chose him to lead his people from Egypt to Canaan, the Promised Land. The Israelites' journey needed a lot of preparation before their departure, which is what the word 'Exodus' means. God was in control of the whole plan including the preparation.

 Too many people

> *After Joseph, his brothers, and everyone else in that generation had died, the people of Israel became so numerous that the whole region of Goshen was full of them. Many years later a new king came to power. He didn't know what Joseph had done for Egypt and he told the Egyptians: "There are too many of those Israelites in our country, and they are becoming more powerful than we are. If we don't outsmart them, their families will keep growing larger. And if our country goes to war, they could easily fight on the side of our enemies and escape from Egypt."*

Exodus 1:6-10

The king of Egypt, Pharaoh, was thought to be descended from the gods and was treated as a god. His words had to be obeyed. A former Pharaoh invited Joseph's family to Egypt during a famine. Joseph's family, the Israelites, loved and followed the true God. God was pleased with them. One way he showed this was that lots of healthy babies were born to the Israelites. A later king came to power in Egypt who did not know about Joseph or his family. The king only saw a big group of people who were not Egyptian. Why was he worried? Was he a good leader? New leaders often bring change. What changes have affected you? (A new government, a new principal or teacher at school, a new boss at work?) Were the changes good or bad? The changes for the Israelites were terrible, but God set about helping them and he chose Moses for the job.

A baby in the reeds

The burning bush

A man from the Levi tribe married a woman from the same tribe, and she later had a baby boy. He was a beautiful child, and she kept him inside for three months. But when she could no longer keep him hidden, she made a basket out of reeds and covered it with tar. She put him in the basket and placed it in the tall grass along the edge of the Nile River. The baby's older sister stood off at a distance to see what would happen to him.

Exodus 2:1-4

It's fun to hide when you're playing. Do you hide when you're afraid or in trouble? This mother hid her tiny baby, Moses, when Pharaoh decided to kill all the Israelite baby boys. Pharaoh was afraid of the growing Israelite population. When the baby could no longer be hidden, the mother made him a waterproof basket. She put him in it, hiding it among the reeds in the river. God's preparation to help his people had begun. He looked after Moses even when he was only a tiny baby. The basket was found by the king's daughter, a princess. She felt sorry for baby Moses because he was crying and hungry and decided to keep him. She found an Israelite mother to look after him.

Thank you God that you have a plan for people who love you. Thank you that nothing can stop your plan.

One day, Moses was taking care of the sheep and goats of his father-in-law Jethro, the priest of Midian, and Moses decided to lead them across the desert to Sinai, the holy mountain. There an angel of the Lord appeared to him from a burning bush. Moses saw that the bush was on fire, but it wasn't burning up. "This is strange!" he said to himself. "I'll go over and see why the bush isn't burning up." When the Lord saw Moses coming near the bush, he called him by name, and Moses answered, "Here I am."

Exodus 3:1-4

What's the most amazing thing you have ever seen? Moses was looking after his father-in-law's sheep at Mt Sinai where there was fresh grass. Then he saw an amazing sight, a burning bush that kept on burning, not burning itself up. It was so unusual that he went to look at it close up. As he walked towards the burning bush the Lord called his name, and told him who it was speaking to him. Moses listened. God told Moses that he knew how cruelly the Israelites were being treated by the Egyptians. Moses' job was to lead the Israelites away to another land. How do you think Moses felt?

Thank you Lord that you speak to your people. Thank you that we have the Bible to read and learn about you. Help us to follow what it says.

3 Sticks into snakes

 # 4 Let my people go

 Moses asked the Lord, "Suppose everyone refuses to listen to my message, and no one believes that you really appeared to me?" The Lord answered, "What's that in your hand?" "A walking stick," Moses replied. "Throw it down!" the Lord commanded. So Moses threw the stick on the ground. It immediately turned into a snake, and Moses jumped back. "Pick it up by the tail!" the Lord commanded. And when Moses did this, the snake turned back into a walking stick.

Exodus 4:1-4

Do you sometimes feel no one listens? Moses was afraid that the Israelites would not listen to him when he told them that God had appeared and spoken to him. To encourage Moses, God gave him a special sign to show to the people. Despite this miracle, Moses pleaded with God to send someone else because he wasn't a good speaker. So God sent Moses' brother, Aaron, with him to speak to the Israelite leaders. Moses showed the powerful signs to the Israelites and they did believe him. The Israelites bowed down and worshipped God. They were thankful that God was going to take them away from the cruel Egyptians.

 Lord, you know when things are difficult for us. Thank you that you will help us when we ask you.

 Moses and Aaron went to the king of Egypt and told him, "The Lord God says, 'Let my people go into the desert so they can honour me with a celebration there.' " "Who is this Lord and why should I obey him?" the king replied. "I refuse to let you and your people go!" They answered, "The Lord God of the Hebrews has appeared to us. Please let us walk for three days into the desert where we can offer sacrifices to him. If you don't, he may strike us down with terrible troubles or with war." The king said, "Moses and Aaron, why are you keeping these people from working? Look how many you are keeping from doing their work. Now everyone get back to work!"

Exodus 5:1-5

Moses and Aaron had to go to the king to tell him God's message. They had to repeat their request. The king was stubborn and became angry. He made the Israelites work even harder. Moses complained to God. 'Why did you send me here? Ever since I went to the king to speak for you, he has treated them cruelly.' But God was in control and bringing his plan into action. He said, 'Now you are going to see what I will do to the king. I will force him to let my people go.'

 Lord God, sometimes it's hard to speak about you. Help us to tell others about your love.

5 Crossing the Red Sea

But Moses answered, "Don't be afraid! Be brave and you will see the Lord save you today. These Egyptians will never bother you again. The Lord will fight for you, and you won't have to do a thing." ... Moses stretched his arm over the sea, and the Lord sent a strong east wind that blew all night until there was dry land where the water had been. The sea opened up, and the Israelites walked through on dry land with a wall of water on each side.

Exodus 14:13-14 and 21-22

The Israelites knew the way to Canaan – out of Egypt and turn left! But God told Moses to go another way, longer but safer. Or was it? 'We've come the wrong way', the Israelites thought as they saw the sea in front, the desert behind, the mountains on either side. Pharaoh heard they were trapped so he set out to capture them. The Israelites were terrified and cried to Moses, 'Why did you bring us out here to die?' What did Moses say? With no time to waste he organised the people on the beach. He climbed on a rock and lifted up his stick as God had told him. How amazing! A path opened up in the sea. All the Israelites crossed safely, then God told Moses to hold out his hand over the sea. The water returned to its normal level.

Dear Lord, when things seem to be going wrong all the time, help us to trust in you.

Merry-go-round the·Bible

Bible heroes - Samuel

10

This story happened more than a thousand years before Jesus. God's people the Israelites were in a bad way and most of them weren't bothering much about God. But God didn't forget them: he chose someone to be a leader, to bring them back to the best way of living. That leader, Samuel, is our hero for this week.

Samuel was a very special leader of God's people. He lived many years as a prophet helping people know about God. He was also a good general and he also acted like a Prime Minister, making laws and governing the people. However, he is remembered best because he loved God and tried to be obedient to him. Eli the High Priest taught him about God and he never forgot that it was God who called him to be a prophet.

A promise made

Elkanah had two wives, Hannah and Peninnah ... Once a year Elkanah travelled from his home town to Shiloh, where he offered sacrifices. Eli was the Lord's priest there... Whenever Elkanah offered a sacrifice, he gave some of the meat to Peninnah and some to each of her sons and daughters. But he gave Hannah even more, because he loved Hannah very much, even though the Lord had kept her from having children of her own.

1 Samuel 1:2-5

Hannah was sad because she hadn't any children. When the Bible was written it was thought that God didn't care about you if you were a married woman without children. But her husband Elkanah showed that he loved her, giving her extra helpings at the once-a-year special meal they had when they went to Shiloh to worship God! Sometimes we love someone, but we don't bother to show them. What are some ways *we* can show people that we love them? (Write them a note, make them a present, spend some time with them? What else?) What can we do this week to show someone how much we love them?

When the sacrifice had been offered, and they had eaten the meal, Hannah got up and went to pray. Eli was sitting in his chair near the door to the place of worship. Hannah was broken-hearted and was crying as she prayed, "Lord All-Powerful, I am your servant, but I am so miser-able! Please let me have a son. I will give him to you for as long as he lives."... Eli (told her) "You may go home now and stop worrying. I'm sure the God of Israel will answer your prayer."

1 Samuel 1:9-11, 17

It was really important to Hannah to have a son. She cried her eyes out to God about it. She had a very loving husband. He cared for her but other women may have been very unkind to her. They may have told her that God didn't really love her. With Eli's help, she was able to trust God and leave the problem in his hands.

Lord our God, thank you that we can be sure that you're always ready to listen to us; we're sorry if sometimes when we pray to you we're not really serious. Help us to think what to pray about, to say what we mean, and to trust you to answer.

2 A promise kept

Later the Lord blessed Elkanah and Hannah with a son. She named him Samuel because she had asked the Lord for him ... When it was the time of year to go to Shiloh again, Hannah and Elkanah took Samuel to the Lord's house ... "Sir," Hannah said (to Eli), "a few years ago I stood here beside you and asked the Lord to give me a child. Here he is! The Lord gave me just what I asked for. Now I am giving him to the Lord, and he will be the Lord's servant for as long as he lives."

1 Samuel 1:19-20, 24, 26-28

Samuel was a special gift from God. That's why Hannah called him Samuel, which means 'Someone from God', or 'Heard by God'. It must have been very hard for her to let go of her precious little boy of about 4 years old, but Hannah didn't forget the promise she had made. She knew that her son would be well cared for. She also knew that if he stayed with Eli he would learn about God and how to serve and obey him. Children don't belong to their parents: parents care for them and love them because they realise that they belong to God.

Thank you Lord that you keep your promises. Help us to keep the ones we make, both to other people and to you.

3 A voice in the night

Samuel served the Lord by helping Eli the priest, who by that time was almost blind. In those days, the Lord hardly ever spoke directly to people, and he didn't appear to them in dreams very often. But one night, Eli was asleep in his room, and Samuel was sleeping on a mat near the sacred chest in the Lord's house. They had not been asleep very long when the Lord called out Samuel's name. "Here I am!" Samuel answered. Then he ran to Eli and said, "Here I am. What do you want?" "I didn't call you," Eli answered. "Go back to bed."

1 Samuel 3:1-5

God rarely spoke directly to people then, probably because they'd stopped listening. But God had a special job for Samuel and so he needed to speak to him directly. Since then, God still 'speaks' to us strongly, clearly and beautifully in the teaching and the life of Jesus. And it's all written down for us in the Bible.

Our Father, you have so many important and lovely things to say to everybody. We're sad about people who don't want to listen to you: help us never to be like that, but to listen for your voice and learn to recognise it.

God's call

 # Samuel speaks for the Lord

 Eli finally realised that it was the Lord who was speaking to Samuel. So he said, "Go back and lie down! If someone speaks to you again, answer, 'I'm listening, Lord. What do you want me to do?'" Once again Samuel went back and lay down. The Lord then stood beside Samuel and called out as he had done before, "Samuel! Samuel!" "I'm listening," Samuel answered. "What do you want me to do?"

1 Samuel 3:8b-10

God spoke to Samuel with a voice that sounded like another person's voice. He still talks to people in this way sometimes. But because, like Samuel, we're not very good at recognising his voice, he's given us a much more reliable way of hearing what he wants to tell us. As we saw yesterday, this is the Bible. Its teaching is God's word on everything that really matters. Just as the food God gives us doesn't do us any good unless we eat it and digest it, the Bible is no help to us unless we hear what it says and put it into practice.

 Thank you Lord, for the Bible. Help us, like Samuel, to listen to what you have to say to us, and to be ready to do what you tell us.

 As Samuel grew up, the Lord helped him and made everything Samuel said come true. From the town of Dan in the north to the town of Beersheba in the south, everyone in the country knew that Samuel was truly the Lord's prophet. The Lord often appeared to Samuel at Shiloh and told him what to say. Then Samuel would speak to the whole nation of Israel.

1 Samuel 3:19-21; 4:1a

This short reading covers perhaps 20 years. As Samuel grew up, he continued as he began, by listening to God and obeying him. This must have been a great joy to Hannah, who prayed that he would be God's person all his life. He didn't just listen to God: he also told other people what God was saying. Because what he said was wise, people recognised that his teaching came from God.

 Thank you Lord, that you speak to us through the Bible and each other. Please give us the courage to share what we learn with others. Help us to know when it is the right moment for this and may our words and lives show we are your people.

11
Bible heroes - David

Many years after the time of last week's story, Samuel was an old man. Israel now had a king called Saul. He'd done some good things but had become proud and foolish. He became so concerned with himself that he began to neglect the people. He became very bad tempered and often flew into fits of rage. Then he would sulk and the king's court had to try to calm him down. His real problem was that he had disobeyed God and he knew it. Disobeying God and not doing anything about it always brings problems. God knew that Saul would not change. He didn't want his people to have a bad king. So he sent Samuel to begin the process of replacing Saul with a king who loved God and would obey him. That special person was David.

 One day (the Lord) said, "Samuel, I've rejected Saul and I refuse to let him be king any longer. Stop feeling sad about him. Put some olive oil in a small container and go and visit a man named Jesse, who lives in Bethlehem. I've chosen one of his sons to be my king." Samuel answered, "If I do that, Saul will find out and have me killed." "Take a calf with you," the Lord replied. "Tell everyone that you've come to offer it as a sacrifice to me, then invite Jesse to the sacrifice. When I show you which one of his sons I have chosen, pour the olive oil on his head." Samuel did what the Lord told him.

1 Samuel 16:1-4a

If you know the end of the story, it seems easy to be brave. But sometimes God asks us to do something hard, and we don't know how it's going to work out. Here Samuel was afraid but he trusted and obeyed God. This Bible verse sums it up — try and learn it this week. Make up a tune and sing it too!

I trust you Lord God,
        and I won't be afraid.
My power and my strength
        come from you.
I trust you Lord God,
        and I won't be afraid.

Isaiah 12:2

David chosen

Jesse presented seven of his sons to Samuel; some of them looked just right to be king. But God told Samuel, *"People judge others by what they look like, but I judge people by what's in their hearts."* ... Samuel said to Jesse, *"Do you have any more sons?" "Yes,"* Jesse answered. *"My youngest son David is out taking care of the sheep." "Send for him!"* Samuel said. ... Jesse sent for David. He was a healthy, good-looking boy with a sparkle in his eyes. As soon as David came, the Lord told Samuel, *"He's the one!"* ... Samuel poured the oil on David's head while his brothers watched. At that moment, the Spirit of the Lord took control of David and stayed with him from then on.*

1 Samuel 16:7, 11-13

The oil was poured on David's head, not to improve his hairstyle but to show he was specially chosen by God. If David hadn't allowed God's Spirit to come into his life and take control of him, the oil on the head would have been of no use.

Lord, you can see what's in our hearts; you can see our selfishness. Please change us – you can see our needs – please give us your Holy Spirit too.

David to the battle

King Saul was often stressed out. His servants suggested that music might help. Saul asked them to find a person who could play the harp well. Someone suggested David.

Saul sent a message to Jesse: "Tell your son David to leave your sheep and come here to me." Jesse loaded a donkey with bread and a goatskin full of wine, then he told David to take the donkey and a young goat to Saul. David went to Saul and started working for him ... David would play his harp. Saul would relax and feel better, and the evil spirit would go away.

1 Samuel 16:19-21, 23

David was tough. Out on the hills with the sheep, he fought and killed lions. But just because he was tough (and a boy!) didn't mean he couldn't write poetry and play songs as well. Some of his songs have been popular for 3,000 years! As we'll see soon, God also used his gift for music to arrange that David was in the right place at the right time.

Thank you Lord for making each one of us good at doing different things. Help us to use these gifts of yours to serve you.

Making fun of God

 # The Lord wins the battle

 Picture the scene: Saul's army and Israel's old enemies the Philistines are facing each other across a valley. Out from the enemy ranks walks Goliath, huge and terrifying. He yells out:

"Here and now I challenge Israel's whole army! Choose someone to fight me!" Saul and his men heard what Goliath said, but they were so frightened of Goliath that they couldn't do a thing ... Then David arrived to see his brothers. While David was talking with them, Goliath came out from the line of Philistines and started boasting as usual. David heard him... (He) asked some soldiers standing nearby ... "Who does that worthless Philistine think he is? He's making fun of the army of the living God."

1 Samuel 17:10-11, 23, 26

Do you ever feel sad when someone with you makes fun of a person in your family or one of your friends? David felt like that about God and he spoke up for him.

 Lord, we pray that when people are proud enough to think that they can make fun of you, we won't be afraid of them. Help us to stand up for you and be strong – and to be wise and loving as well.

 (David) went out to a stream and picked up five smooth stones and put them in his leather bag. Then with his sling in his hand, he went straight towards Goliath. Goliath then swore at David to try to make him feel small and cursed him. *David answered: "You've come out to fight me with a sword and a spear and a dagger. But I've come out to fight you in the name of the Lord All-Powerful. He is the God of Israel's army, and you have insulted him too! Today the Lord will help me defeat you... Then the whole world will know that Israel has a real God."*

1 Samuel 17:40, 45-46

David knew he was a crack shot with a sling. But as he walked up the hill towards Goliath, it wasn't the sling he trusted. It was God. When we're under pressure, there are many things that can help: our quick thinking, physical strength, common sense, friends, family etc. But real power and strength comes from God. Do you remember the memory verse you learned at the weekend?

 We're so glad, Father God, that you're for us and that we can rely on you. When we need help, help us to turn to you first, not just when everything else has failed.

David kills Goliath

When Goliath started forward, David ran towards him. He put a stone in his sling and swung the sling around by its straps. When he let go of one strap, the stone flew out and hit Goliath on the forehead. It cracked his skull, and he fell face down on the ground. David defeated Goliath with a sling and a stone. He killed him without even using a sword.

1 Samuel 17:48-50

Festo Kivengere of Uganda was a great man and a wonderful Christian. His gifts were used by God to stir the hearts and minds of thousands of people all over the world. How did he become a Christian? A primary school girl told him (a grown man, a teacher) that Jesus loved him! God loves to use the things that seem weak, like stones from stream beds and prayer and humble service and quiet words and a crucified saviour, to show up the strong, the noisy and the proud. David learnt this lesson when he defeated Goliath. The lesson to trust in God's strength remained with him all his life.

Lord what a wonderful and surprising God you are! Help us to see things as you see them and to trust you always.

Life as it should be
12

Lent 1

Do you know what Lent is? Lent is a special time to think about the death of Jesus. It begins on a day we call Ash Wednesday and lasts for 40 days. It ends just before Easter. This week we are going to look at some of the advice Jesus gave to people so they would know how to live as Christians. You see if we want to please Jesus, who died for us, we should live the way he suggests. It won't always be easy, but it will be the best way. If we accept this advice we will be specially ready for Easter. We will know what Easter is really about.

The law

 # Depend on him

Don't suppose that I came to do away with the Law and the Prophets. I didn't come to do away with them, but to give them their full meaning. Heaven and earth may disappear. But I promise you that not even a full stop or comma will ever disappear from the Law. Everything written in it must happen.

Matthew 5:17-18

When Jesus was talking about the Law and Prophets he meant most of the Old Testament. Long before Jesus was born as a baby, prophets (people who were God's messengers) spoke about him. A prophet called Micah told people the place where he would be born. Another prophet called Isaiah told people that he would die. We can be sure that everything written about Jesus will happen. We can depend on it. As far as the Law is concerned, it is summarised in the rules called the Ten Commandments. Jesus is saying that he can tell us what the commandments really mean.

This week look up the Ten Commandments in Exodus 20. Make a poster about one of them and put it on the refrigerator.

God blesses those people who depend only on him. They belong to the kingdom of heaven! God blesses those people who grieve. They will find comfort! God blesses those people who are humble. The earth will belong to them!

Matthew 5:3-5

What's an independent person? An independent person thinks and does things for themselves. One day a two year old girl called Sally loudly and proudly announced to some visitors, 'I'm wearing big girl underpants.' Her mother was very embarrassed but was glad her daughter was finally out of nappies and becoming independent in that way. So becoming independent is a good thing. But in one way it isn't. The opposite of independence is dependence. All our lives we need to be dependent on God. Depending on God means relying on him to provide the things we need and asking him for help whenever we have a problem. If anyone says you don't need God's help, they're wrong. We all need it. So let's try and be independent in some ways but dependent on God always.

Father, may we never forget that we need to depend on you every day of our lives.

Obey him

 # Be happy

 God blesses those people who want to obey him more than to eat or drink. They will be given what they want! God blesses those people who are merciful. They will be treated with mercy! God blesses those people whose hearts are pure. They will see him! God blesses those people who make peace. They will be called his children!

Matthew 5:6-9

 God blesses those people who are treated badly for doing right. They belong to the kingdom of heaven. God will bless you when people insult you, mistreat you, and tell all kinds of evil lies about you because of me. Be happy and excited! You will have a great reward in heaven. People did these same things to the prophets who lived long ago.

Matthew 5:10-12

All the readings for this week are taken from the special talk that Jesus gave on the side of a mountain. Sometimes we call this talk the Beatitudes – or the 'Be-attitudes'. You see, Jesus talked about the sort of attitudes we should have if we call ourselves God's children. The Bible talks about children, fathers and mothers. We are told that children should obey their parents. Well, if we call God our father, we should obey him too. Some people have the attitude that obeying God isn't important. Sooner or later they will find out that this brings unhappiness for themselves and others. You see, God's ways are loving and kind, not selfish. If we have the attitude that obeying God is best, we'll make ourselves and others much happier.

 Help us Father to have the right attitudes and always to obey you.

What makes you happy? Birthdays, Christmas, holidays, chocolates? How do you feel when people tell lies about you, or call you names or treat you badly? Jesus said be happy and excited when those bad things happen. What did he mean? Well, if people treat us badly because we behave badly, we only have ourselves to blame. But if we are treated badly because we are Christians we can be glad. We may feel hurt about it, but one day God will make it all worthwhile. Happiness is not just things, people or places making us feel good. Happiness is when we know that what we are doing is right. The Bible sometimes uses the little word called JOY to describe this. We can be full of joy even when people treat us badly because we know God is with us and pleased with us.

 Father, forgive us if we have behaved badly. But if we are treated badly because we are Christians, please help us.

Salt of
the earth

Light for
the world

You are like salt for everyone on earth. But if salt no longer tastes like salt, how can it make food salty? All it's good for is to be thrown out and walked on.

Matthew 5:13

Years ago, if you wanted to buy a packet of chips there were only two flavours – plain or salt and vinegar. These days there are many flavours. Most contain salt. If they didn't they wouldn't taste as good! When Jesus said that Christians are like salt, what do you think he meant? Do we make things taste better? Not exactly. He meant that we make life better for everyone else. If we try to live the same loving, serving way that Jesus did, we will improve our communities. If you have salt but never pour it out of the salt shaker it won't flavour anything. No one benefits from it. So with us, whenever possible we must try and be friends with people in our streets, schools, clubs and workplaces and try to make life better for them.

Help us Jesus, not to keep your love to ourselves but to share it with others so that life is better for them.

You are like light for the whole world. A city built on top of a hill can't be hidden, and no one would light a lamp and put it under a clay pot. A lamp is placed on a lampstand, where it can give light to everyone in the house. Make your light shine, so that others will see the good that you do and will praise your Father in heaven.

Matthew 5:14-16

It's a dark night. Imagine you're camping in a tent. You hear a noise. You grab your torch. You switch it on. No light! The batteries are flat – the torch is useless. Jesus talks about useless lights. We should be like a light that shines brightly and show God's love in the way we live. If people ask you, be ready to tell them what you believe. In a dark room, a light helps us see what is really there. We can help others to see that Jesus is really there. Make sure that your light keeps on shining. Stay close to God, praying and learning from the Bible. Imagine you are the torch and that prayer and Bible reading are your batteries. If you don't pray and read the Bible the batteries will go flat and your light will not shine. Think about it.

Dear Jesus, may we never hide our love for you. Help us to be like shining lights that point others to you.

Obedience

13

T *his week is a chance to learn more from Jesus. The best way to learn how to build a house is to be ·prenticed to an experienced ·ilder. A good builder knows the ·rious stages of construction and ·w to make the building safe.*

·ilding lives is a bit like building ·uses. The best way is to be an ·prentice with Jesus. (The Bible ·lls apprentices 'disciples'.) He ·ows best because he made us in ·e first place. He also knows the ·st way to live because of the way ·lived. He came to earth to show ·how. That was a fantastic thing ·do. As we get ready for Easter, ·e will spend some time learning ·w we can live like Jesus.

 Sand and rock

> *Anyone who hears and obeys these teachings of mine is like a wise person who built a house on solid rock. Rain poured down, rivers flooded, and winds beat against that house. But it didn't fall, because it was built on solid rock. Anyone who hears my teachings and doesn't obey them is like a foolish person who built a house on sand. The rain poured down, rivers flooded and the winds blew and beat against that house. Finally it fell with a crash.*
>
> Matthew 7:24-27

There is no point building a house on the edge of a river or on an old rubbish tip. Good builders choose stable ground and make sure by pouring concrete for foundations, usually adding steel mesh as well. In Jesus' story, two builders build houses. A violent storm lashes the buildings but only one survives because it is built on a strong flat rock. The things Jesus taught are like such a rock or like concrete foundations. His teaching will keep our lives safe ... if we listen carefully and obey what he tells us. But if we ignore what Jesus tells us, we might as well build our lives on sand which blows around or mud which moves and sinks.

This weekend let's build a model house out of Lego, or blocks, or boxes to remind us of Jesus' story. Is someone building a new house on a block near us? We could go and have a look at the progress the builder is making. Has he poured the foundations yet?

Giving

 Praying

 When you do good deeds, don't try to show off. If you do, you won't get a reward from your Father in heaven. When you give to the poor, don't blow your own trumpet. That's what show-offs do in the meeting places and on the street corners, because they are always looking for praise. I can assure you that they already have their reward. When you give to the poor, don't let anyone know about it.

Matthew 6:1-3

What sort of things can we give to others? We can give them our time. For example, if a very old person is sick they might like us to read to them. We can give money or food or clothes. We can give help. We can even give advice. How do we give? Some members of the community in Jesus' day were known as the Pharisees, because they were very careful to know and keep all God's rules. Some of them were show-offs. When they prayed or gave things to others, they wanted everyone to notice. Jesus said we were not to be like that. Let's give to others but not so that people will look at us and think we're great. Let's give because we really do care about the people we're trying to help.

 Dear Jesus, help us to give to others who are in need. Help us not to be show-offs.

 When you pray, don't be like those show-offs who love to stand up and pray in the meeting places and on the street corners. They do this just to look good. I can assure you that they already have their reward. When you pray, go into a room alone and close the door. Pray to your Father in private. He knows what's done in private, and he will reward you. When you pray, don't talk on and on as people do who don't know God. They think God likes to hear long prayers.

Matthew 6:5-7

Was Jesus impressed by show-offs? One of the wonderful things about God is that he accepts us just as we are and we don't have to try and impress him. Jesus told a story about two men who prayed in the temple. One prayed proudly and boastfully. The other said a very short quiet prayer telling God how sorry he was for his sins. God was more pleased with that prayer. Notice that Jesus says 'when' you pray, not 'if' you pray. Think of all the things we do everyday – eating, sleeping, working, playing, relaxing and so on. Well, prayer should be in there too, a natural part of every day. God loves us and wants us to pray to him.

 God our Father, in our busy days help us to remember to pray. Thank you that we don't have to impress you when we pray.

Example of prayer

You should pray like this: Our Father in heaven, help us to honour your name. Come and set up your kingdom, so that everyone on earth will obey you, as you are obeyed in heaven. Give us our food for today. Forgive us for doing wrong, as we forgive others. Keep us from being tempted and protect us from evil.

Matthew 6:9-13

This is called the Lord's prayer because our Lord Jesus said it. Let's look at four things in this prayer – help us, give us, forgive us, and keep us. Pretend you are drawing a square. As you draw one side say 'help us', as you draw the next side say 'give us'. For the next say 'forgive us' and as you draw the last side say 'keep us'. Your square is complete. Of course as we say those words we must try to remember what Jesus meant by them. 'Help us' is about asking God to help us to put him first in everything we do. 'Give us' means asking for things we really need. 'Forgive us' means we are sorry for the wrong things we have done asking him to forgive us. 'Keep us' means asking God for help to stay on his track and remain safe.

Our Father in heaven, please help us, give us, forgive us and keep us always.

Forgiving

If you forgive others for the wrongs they do to you, your Father in heaven will forgive you. But if you don't forgive others, your Father won't forgive your sins.

Matthew 6:14-15

Imagine a ball of wool tightly wound and tangled up in knots? You try to unravel it but it won't unwind. In a way that's how we become if we don't forgive others. If someone hurts us in some way and we don't forgive them, we keep on thinking about them and what they did. Before we know it all our thoughts about them are twisted and tangled like that ball of wool. Those thoughts stop us enjoying the good things God has given us. No wonder God tells us to forgive others. But forgiving others is not just to make ourselves feel better but it passes on the love that we have received from God. God loves us and will forgive us. Let's love others and forgive them.

Dear Jesus, thank you that you forgive us. Help us to forgive others even when it is hard.

⑤ Fasting

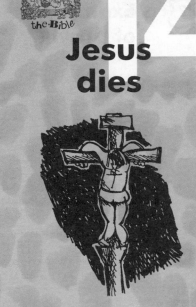

When you go without eating, don't try to look gloomy as those show-offs do when they go without eating. I can assure you that they already have their reward. Instead, comb your hair and wash your face. Then others won't know that you are going without eating. But your Father sees what's done in private, and he will reward you.

Matthew 6:16-18

Fasting usually means going without food for a time so we can pray instead. Sometimes we go without food to lose weight! But that's not what Jesus means. Fasting is a loving thing to do; the person fasting gives up something they like to show their love to God. They often spend the time praying to God for others. Again, Jesus tells us not to show off by telling everyone about it and going around with a long face looking hungry and glum. If you feel God wants you to fast but you don't like the idea of not eating, maybe you could fast in another way. Perhaps you could give up watching TV for a while or not sleep in and spend that time in prayer. Whatever we do, it should be for the right reasons, not to be show-offs.

 Father, help us to be ready to give up something so we can spend that time in prayer.

Jesus dies

Easter 1

T he readings for this week are sad and make us thoughtful. We will remember how Jesus' friends let him down and how his enemies hurt him. Yet through all this, Jesus still loved people. Even at the end of his life, he only wanted to do what his father expected. He was betrayed by someone who was his friend and then sent to his death by people who should have known better.

This week, let's think about Jesus dying on the cross and ask ourselves, 'What do we think about that?'

Betrayed

 Around midday, the sky turned dark and stayed that way until the middle of the afternoon. The sun stopped shining, and the curtain in the temple split down the middle. Jesus shouted, "Father, I put myself in your hands!" Then he died. When the Roman officer saw what had happened, he praised God and said, "Jesus must really have been a good man!"

Luke 23:44-49

This too is a week of very sad readings. Jesus was betrayed, insulted, brought to court, sentenced to death and crucified. When he finally died, it was the saddest time the world had ever known. Imagine the scene: daylight mysteriously turns to darkness; people grope in the dark wondering what it means. Jesus' enemies are glad he is dead. Jesus' mother and followers are dismayed. All their hopes are gone. They are very sad. The Roman soldier realises that Jesus didn't deserve to die, but it is too late. Jesus is dead and the darkness seems to have won.

We could make a picture or model of the cross this weekend. And who will write or copy a prayer, poem or words to a song to place near the cross. (More than one can.)

 Jesus spoke to the chief priests, the temple police, and the leaders who had come to arrest him. He said, "Why do you come out with swords and clubs and treat me like a criminal? I was with you every day in the temple, and you didn't arrest me. But this is your time, and darkness is in control."

Luke 22:52-53

Who knows the name of the disciple who betrayed Jesus? It was Judas. Like each of us, Judas had a choice: he could choose or refuse to love Jesus. He chose not to love him because money was more important than Jesus. For thirty pieces of silver, Judas told Jesus' enemies where they could find him. Jesus was in the garden of Gethsemane praying with some of his disciples. When the enemies came with all their weapons, it looked like they'd come to arrest a dangerous robber rather than Jesus. Jesus is sometimes called the light of the world. He is full of goodness and love. When he was betrayed, it seemed as if the bad things were winning so Jesus said, 'Darkness is in command.' We know that darkness did not win, but a long night of sadness was ahead.

 It makes us sad Lord Jesus to remember that someone you loved betrayed you. May we never turn against you.

Mocked

 # Tried

The men who were guarding Jesus made fun of him and beat him. They put a blindfold on him and said, "Tell us who struck you!" They kept on insulting Jesus in many other ways.

Luke 22:63-65

When we read verses like this, with Jesus being insulted and made fun of, it helps to think about who he really is. The Bible tells us that in the very beginning he created the world (Colossians 1:16). Graham Kendrick wrote a song about Jesus called 'The Servant King'. It says that his hands 'flung stars into space'. Jesus is far more great and powerful than we can ever imagine. Yet here people were making fun of Jesus. The man they blindfolded was the one who gave words of love and comfort to so many others. Sometimes we laugh at people. We make fun of them because everyone else is. We want to follow the crowd. Think. If you had been with the soldiers that night when they made fun of Jesus, would you have joined in?

Dear Jesus, you were insulted. You were made fun of. You were mocked. We are sorry the people did this to you. We might have too.

Everyone in the council got up and led Jesus off to Pilate. They started accusing him and said, "We caught this man trying to get our people to riot and to stop paying taxes to the Emperor. He also claims that he is the Messiah, our king." Pilate asked Jesus, "Are you the king of the Jews?"

"Those are your words," Jesus answered.

Luke 23:1-3

Pilate was the Roman governor, a very important man. Because Jesus' enemies wanted Jesus to be killed, they told Pilate lies about him. Jesus never told people to stop paying taxes to the Emperor. He never tried to get people to riot. What should Pilate do? He didn't know: he didn't think Jesus should be killed but Jesus' enemies were very persistent. Pilate was confused and scared. If he pleased Jesus' enemies an innocent man would be put to death. Of all the people we have ever read about, Pontius Pilate is one of the saddest. He just couldn't make up his mind about Jesus. Each one of us has to make up our minds about Jesus. Will we love and follow him? Will we turn away from him?

Dear Lord Jesus, may we love and follow you all of our lives.

Condemned

 # Crucified

 The people kept on shouting as loud as they could for Jesus to be put to death. Finally, Pilate gave in. He freed the man who was in jail for rioting and murder, because he was the one the crowd wanted to be set free. Then Pilate handed Jesus over for them to do what they wanted with him.

Luke 23:23-25

Finally Pilate made up his mind. It was a difficult decision for him but it shows it was more important for him to please people than it was to please God. So he said, 'Yes, Jesus can be executed.' A swap was made between Jesus and another prisoner. Barabbas was to be set free and Jesus put to death. It seems all wrong and upside down. Jesus, who had never done anything wrong was to be killed. Yet Barabbas who was a murderer and troublemaker was set free. It was so unfair. Perhaps Jesus' enemies thought they had what they wanted. Perhaps they thought they'd won. They were wrong!

 Lord God, help us to want to please you more than people.

 Two criminals were led out to be put to death with Jesus. When the soldiers came to the place called "The Skull", they nailed Jesus to a cross. They also nailed the two criminals to crosses, one on each side of Jesus. Jesus said, "Father, forgive these people! They don't know what they're doing." While the crowd stood there watching Jesus, the soldiers gambled for his clothes. The leaders insulted him by saying, "He saved others. Now he should save himself, if he really is God's chosen Messiah."

Luke 23:32-35

Imagine you'd watched Jesus die at that sad and ugly place. You saw our Saviour dying along with two robbers on crosses, while soldiers played games to win his clothes. Some important people teased Jesus and dared him to save himself. How painful for him. How humiliating that people made fun of him while he was dying. Yet even when he suffered, he thought about others. All his life he acted in loving ways and now he showed love to his worst enemies, praying that God his Father would forgive them. Great pain did not stop great love.

 Lord Jesus, you are such an example to us. Even when your enemies hurt you and made fun of you, you asked God to forgive them. Thank you for your great love for all people.

15

Jesus is risen

Easter 2

*T**his is the best week ever!
It starts with darkness and
despair and ends with
happiness and joy. All the
sadness turns to happiness as the
followers of Jesus discover that
Jesus is not dead – he is very
much alive. 'He is risen' is the
oldest saying in the church. Watch
out and see if anyone says this in
your church on Easter Sunday
morning. Even if they don't, say
it to each other as you get ready
to go to church yourselves.*

WE Understanding

*Then [Jesus] helped them
understand the Scriptures. He told
them, "The Scriptures say that the
Messiah must suffer, then three
days later he will rise from death.
They also say that all people of
every nation must be told in my
name to turn to God, in order to
be forgiven. So beginning in
Jerusalem, you must tell everyone
everything that has happened.
I will send you the one my Father
has promised, but you must stay
in the city until you are given
power from heaven."*

Luke 24:45-49

Imagine that the person you love most
goes away and you know you will
never see them again. Then unexpect-
edly they return. You'd hardly believe
it was true. That's how it was when
Jesus came alive again. Then he was
able to help his friends understand
what it all meant and some people
wrote this down in the Bible. Today,
the Holy Spirit helps us understand
everything we read there about Jesus
– his life for us, his death for us and his
coming alive again for us. All for us!

Why not make a poster this weekend
and put it on the fridge. Use words
which tell us what Jesus did for us,
such as: 'And I now live by faith in the
Son of God, who loved me and gave his
life for me.' (Galatians 2:20b)

Jesus buried

 ## Waiting

 Joseph went to Pilate and asked for Jesus' body. He took the body down from the cross and wrapped it in fine cloth. Then he put it in a tomb that had been cut out of solid rock and had never been used.

Luke 23:52-53

Joseph was a member of the Jewish council. Jesus told people that their inward thoughts and care of others mattered more to God than being proud of keeping the outward religious rules. Although the leaders were good at rule keeping Jesus kept showing them they were two-faced. This annoyed the councillors and most were probably glad Jesus was dead. But Joseph, a secret follower of Jesus, hadn't wanted Jesus to die. He wasn't brave enough to share this with his fellow councillors. Now Jesus was dead and it was too late. All Joseph could do for his dead Lord was to take care of his body. The custom was to wrap the body in strips of cloth with spices and place it in a cave or tomb. Joseph never dreamed that the tomb he had ready for himself would be used for the burial of God's son. After the burial, a stone was rolled against the entrance. As Joseph did these things, perhaps he felt sad, angry and disappointed that he hadn't been brave enough earlier to show he loved Jesus.

 Dear Jesus, may we never be too scared to tell others we love you and follow you. Help us to be brave even when it is difficult.

 The women who had come with Jesus from Galilee followed Joseph and watched how Jesus' body was placed in the tomb. Then they went to prepare some sweet-smelling spices for his burial. But on the Sabbath day they rested, as the Law of Moses commands.

Luke 23:55-56

Immediately after a death, women prepared the body properly for burial with spices. On this Friday, there was not enough time for this before the Sabbath started. What stopped the women was God's law. The law said no one should work on the Sabbath day. So the day after Jesus was buried must have seemed the longest day ever for Jesus' followers. God's laws are given for good reasons. By not working on the Sabbath day, the women were able to rest quietly, to cry and pray. God gives us times to be quiet and to rest. This helps our bodies to get the extra rest they need so we have strength for what's ahead. Jesus' women friends came on the Sunday to complete the preparations for his proper burial. The women thought they would need strength and courage to walk to the tomb, move the huge stone, then properly prepare his body with spices. Little did they know they would need strength for something far more wonderful.

 We thank you Father, that in our lives you give us times to rest and be quiet so we can gain strength and courage.

Confused

 Remembering

 Very early on Sunday morning, the women went to the tomb carrying the spices that they had prepared. When they found the stone rolled away from the entrance, they went in. But they didn't find the body of the Lord Jesus and they didn't know what to think.

Luke 24:1-4a

Who moved the stone? The women would have been puzzled. But what really upset and confused them was that Jesus' body was missing. Who could have taken it? It didn't make sense. What might have run through their minds? The least they could have hoped for was that he be left in peace in his grave after all that had happened to him, their Lord and master. But they had already forgotten what Jesus told them weeks before. He said he would die but that was not the end. These confused, upset women were about to have a meeting they would never forget.

 Dear Lord Jesus, we are so glad that death was not the end for you. Help us remember the things we know about you.

 Suddenly two men in shining white clothes stood beside them. The women were afraid and bowed to the ground. But the men said, "Why are you looking in the place of the dead for someone who is alive? Jesus isn't here. He's been raised from death. Remember that while he was still in Galilee, he told you, 'The Son of Man will be handed over to sinners who will nail him to a cross. But three days later he will rise to life.' " Then they remembered what Jesus had said.

Luke 24:4-8

Have you played the game 'hot and cold'? You look for something and people call out 'cold' if you're far away or 'hot' if you're near. We could say 'cold' to these women because they were looking in the wrong place for Jesus. It wasn't a game. It was frightening and confusing. First no stone, then no body, then two surprising angels. But the angels brought the best news ever! When we are frightened or confused, it's good to remember what we know of Jesus. The angels reminded the women that Jesus said he would come alive again. Everything began to make sense. Jesus wasn't in a tomb because he was alive!

 Lord Jesus, when we are afraid and confused, help us to remember all that you have said and done. Thank you for coming alive for us.

5 Wondering

Mary Magdalene, Joanna, Mary the mother of James, and some other women were the ones who had gone to the tomb. When they returned, they told the eleven apostles and the others what had happened. The apostles thought it was all nonsense, and they wouldn't believe it. But Peter ran to the tomb. And when he stooped down and looked in, he saw only the burial clothes. Then he returned, wondering what had happened.

Luke 24:9-12

'That's a load of rubbish! It's too good to be true! Tell me another one!' Imagine how these women felt? There they were with the best news of all and the men thought it was nonsense! Until of course one of them went to find out for himself. There in front of Peter were the cloths Joseph had wrapped around Jesus' dead body. But what were they doing there? Peter began to wonder, 'Could it possibly be true?' Like the others, he had forgotten most of the things that Jesus had said before he died. At last Peter realised that a person who is alive does not need grave clothes. A person alive does not stay in a tomb. Jesus is alive!

Lord we thank you for the excitement of that first Easter morning when people discovered you were alive!

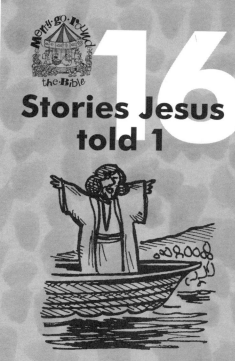

Merry-go-round the Bible

Stories Jesus told 1 16

What's your favourite TV story or video? Young children enjoy hearing their favourite story over and over again. Jesus often told stories. The stories were always interesting to listen to because they had a special meaning. Jesus used to let the people who listened to him work out the meaning for themselves. Some people found the meaning easy to understand, but some couldn't understand it at all. For those who could understand, the story helped them remember the meaning.

Sometimes the story gave advice or a warning or was followed by a lesson. These Bible stories are called parables. Jesus got the ideas for his parables from nature, from everyday life and customs, and from well known events in history.

Keep on praying

 Jesus' disciples asked him what the story meant. So he answered: "I have explained the secrets about God's kingdom to you, but for others I can only use stories. These people look, but they don't see, and they hear, but they don't understand."

Luke 8:9-10

Have you ever said, 'Huh, I don't get it!' when someone tells you a joke or a riddle? When it is explained, you then laugh or sometimes you still don't understand it. Jesus told a parable about a farmer. Afterwards the disciples asked him what it meant as they didn't get the meaning. Jesus told them that his parable explained to them some of God's plans for the future. Until then, no one else knew anything about them. Those who believed would understand but those who refused Jesus' message wouldn't get the meaning.

This weekend we could have a great time telling each other jokes. Here's one to start: 'What do you get if you cross a cat with a laughing hyena?' Answer: 'A giggle puss.' Here's another: 'What do you get if you cross a chicken with an alarm clock?' Answer: 'An alarm chick.'

 Then Jesus went on to say; "Suppose one of you goes to a friend in the middle of the night and says, 'Let me borrow three loaves of bread. A friend of mine has dropped in, and I haven't got anything for him to eat.' And suppose your friend answers, 'Don't bother me! The door is bolted, and my children and I are in bed. I can't get up to give you anything.' He may not get up and give you the bread, just because you are his friend. But he will get up and give you as much as you need, simply because you aren't ashamed to keep on asking."

Luke 11:5-8

What do you say when you plead with Mum and Dad for something, or to go somewhere? Here, this man needs bread to feed some unexpected visitors. He goes to his friend's house in the middle of the night and keeps banging on the door until the friend wakes up. The man is determined to keep banging and calling. The friend finally gives in and hands him some bread just because the man was persistent and would not give up asking. Jesus told this parable to tell the people and us how to pray to him. We are to be persistent. We are to keep on asking in our prayers until God answers.

 Lord help us not to give up praying. Thank you that you hear our prayers and answer them.

Wise and foolish builders

"Anyone who comes and listens to me and obeys me is like someone who dug down deep and built a house on solid rock. When the flood came and the river rushed against the house, it was built so well that it didn't even shake. But anyone who hears what I say and doesn't obey me is like someone whose house wasn't built on solid rock. As soon as the river rushed against that house, it was smashed to pieces!"

Luke 6:47-49

In the city big machines often drill down into rock, making huge foundation holes for buildings that will rise high above ground level. It would take a lot to knock down these buildings! Jesus' story compares two builders. One wise builder built his house on solid rock. When a flood came it wasn't washed away because it was built properly on strong foundations. But the other builder was foolish. He didn't take the time or effort to build properly. What will happen to his house in a flood? People who are wise learn about Jesus and do what he says. They are able to go through difficult times. Those who are foolish hear about Jesus but refuse to follow his ways. They will find it difficult when hard times come.

Jesus, thank you that you are like the wise man's rock. Help us to trust in you.

Speck and logs

"Can one blind person lead another blind person? Won't they both fall into a ditch? Are students better than their teacher? But when they are fully trained, they will be like their teacher. You can see the speck in your friend's eye. But you don't notice the log in your own eye. How can you say, 'My friend, let me take the speck out of your eye,' when you don't see the log in your own eye? You show-offs! First, get the log out of your own eye. Then you can see how to take the speck out of your friend's eye."

Luke 6:39b-42

Do children in your class or your workmates tease one another when they make a mistake? We're often quick to point out other people's mistakes and tease them. How do you feel when someone does this to you? Jesus teaches that his followers must be prepared to learn. Two blind people can't help each other. They must depend on people with sight to guide and teach them. Students must be prepared to learn from their teacher. We must learn to see the big faults in ourselves before we see the little ones in others. We're all learning about Jesus, and whether we're young or old, he is everyone's teacher.

Dear Jesus, forgive us when we have teased others. Thank you that you teach us about God and how to live for him.

See the light

 # Light everywhere

 "No one lights a lamp and puts it under a bowl or under a bed. A lamp is always put on a lampstand, so that people who come into a house will see the light. There is nothing hidden that won't be found."

Luke 8:16-17

Can you remember if we have ever had a blackout at our house? What did we do? How did we feel? (If this hasn't happened an older family member could retell a time when a blackout occurred.) Who groped around in the dark to find a candle and matches or a torch? Where did we put the light? On a table? Where was the best place we found for the little bit of light so it shone out for everyone? Even when there's no blackout, it's no good hiding light. Lights are made to take away the darkness. Jesus uses this picture of the purpose of light to talk about himself to his disciples and the people. He tells them they may not understand everything about him yet. As time goes on he will tell them more about himself. One day they will fully understand Jesus and why God sent him. In the Bible, the whole of God's plan and why Jesus came to earth can be found. But it's up to us to find out more.

 Thank you God for the Bible. Thank you that it tells us of your plan to love us.

 "No one lights a lamp and then hides it or puts it under a clay pot. A lamp is put on a lampstand, so that everyone who comes into the house can see the light. Your eyes are the lamp for your body. When your eyes are good, you have all the light you need. But when your eyes are bad, everything is dark. So be sure that your light isn't darkness. If you have light, and nothing is dark, then light will be everywhere, as when a lamp shines brightly on you."

Luke 11:33-36

Who's played the game 'I spy'? You look around trying to guess what the other person has seen. In this parable, Jesus says our eyes are like a lamp to our body. Whatever we look at affects who we are and what we think, learn and understand about people, things and situations. We can use our eyes to look at good things or we can look at bad things which will seem gloomy and dark. God is pleased with us when we choose good things to look at and do. He wants us to help others see good things too so that there can be light everywhere! What are some good things we can look at?

 Lord Jesus, help us to look at and understand good things. Help us too to share good things with others.

17

And the Spirit came

entecost

*T*his week we will be learning about the first Christian
church. All sorts of different
people were in that church
Jerusalem. If you look at your
urch you too will find all sorts
different people. You would need
be brave to be in the first church
cause Jesus' enemies were angry
people who followed Jesus. The
emies thought Jesus was dead
t he was very much alive in
aven with his Father. But the
urch wasn't alone. God would
nd someone to be with them
rever. So, let's see what happened
these first Christians.

 WE. Tell everyone

*While the apostles were still with
Jesus, they asked him, "Lord, are
you now going to give Israel its
own king again?" Jesus said to
them, "You don't need to know the
time of those events that only the
Father controls. But the Holy
Spirit will come upon you and
give you power. Then you will tell
everyone about me in Jerusalem,
in all Judea, in Samaria, and
everywhere in the world."*

Acts 1:6-8

Have we had some great news lately?
Some people can't wait to tell their
news. Some children say, 'Look my
tooth has come out!' Somehow when
you get older this isn't something you
want to share! God sent the Holy Spirit
so Jesus' followers could have power
to tell everyone the great news about
Jesus. There will come times when
God wants us to tell others about
Jesus. If we are willing to do this,
the Holy Spirit will give us the courage
and whatever else we need so that
we can do it.

The Bible verses talk about telling
people in different countries about
Jesus. Who can think of someone who
has gone to another country to do this?
Can we pray for them and perhaps
write them a letter?

The Spirit came

 # Everyone heard

 On the day of Pentecost all the Lord's followers were together in one place. Suddenly there was a noise from heaven like the sound of a mighty wind! It filled the house where they were meeting. Then they saw what looked like fiery tongues moving in all directions, and a tongue came and settled on each person there. The Holy Spirit took control of everyone, and they began speaking whatever language the Spirit let them speak.

Acts 2:1-4

 Many religious Jews from every country in the world were living in Jerusalem. And when they heard this noise, a crowd gathered. But they were surprised, because they were hearing everything in their own languages. They were excited and amazed and said, "Don't all these who are speaking come from Galilee? Then why do we hear them speaking our very own languages?"

Acts 2:5-8

Everyone has a birthday and so does the Christian church! It is called Pentecost. Up to then, God's Holy Spirit had only been sent to certain people at special times. God promised that after Jesus went to heaven, the Holy Spirit would come to all his followers. The Holy Spirit came in an amazing and wonderful way. It seems strange to us, but it reminds us how awesome God is. He does things in ways we would never imagine. On that day, it was as if the church was born and it has kept growing ever since. We look back at Pentecost thankful that God sent the Holy Spirit. We can also be thankful that all Christians have the Holy Spirit today.

There is a game where a message is whispered around a circle. By the time the message gets to the end, it sounds all 'gobbledy gook'. On the day of Pentecost people may have thought Jesus' followers were speaking 'gobbledy gook' until they listened carefully and realised 'Hey, I can hear them talking in my own language and they are talking about Jesus!' God wanted more people to know about Jesus so he sent the Holy Spirit on a day when foreign visitors were in Jerusalem. The Spirit gave Jesus' followers the ability to speak in other languages so the visitors could easily hear and understand about Jesus. Ever since that time, more and more people have heard about Jesus and that includes us!

 Thank you God that you sent the Holy Spirit in such a wonderful way to help the church to grow. We love belonging to your church.

 God, we are so thankful that we can hear Jesus in our own language. Please help all people who translate the Bible to other languages.

Drink

Everyone was excited and con-
fused. Some of them even kept
asking each other, "What does this
all mean?" Others made fun of the
Lord's followers and said, "They
are drunk."

Acts 2:12b-13

It's an awful feeling when someone
makes fun or tells lies about you.
That's what happened to Jesus' followers. There they were, excitedly telling
people about Jesus in languages they
had never learnt! The Holy Spirit
helped them do this so more people
could hear about Jesus. Then came the
party poopers, the dobbers, the tell
tales: 'Jesus' followers are drunk!' they
cried. 'Don't take any notice of what
they say.' This wasn't true. Sometimes
people say things about Christians that
are unfair or untrue. If this ever
happens to us, we can remember that
it happened to Jesus and his followers.
We are not alone. Besides, if we are
treated badly because we are doing
what God wants, we will be the
winners in the end because we are
on the right side.

Dear Jesus, you know what it
was like to have others tell lies
about you. Help us to follow
you even when it is hard.

Nine o'clock in the morning

Peter stood with the eleven
apostles and spoke in a loud clear
voice to the crowd: "Friends and
everyone else living in Jerusalem,
listen carefully to what I have to
say! You are wrong to think these
people are drunk. After all, it's
only nine o'clock in the morning.
But this is what God had the
prophet Joel say, "When the last
days come, I will give my Spirit to
everyone. Your sons and daughters
will prophesy. Your young men
will see visions and your old men
will have dreams. In those days I
will give my Spirit to my servants,
both men and women, and they
will prophesy."

Acts 2:14-18

A few weeks before this, Peter was a
different man. He was a fisherman who
enthusiastically followed Jesus but
when Jesus was arrested, Peter was a
runaway coward. After Jesus died then
came back to life, Peter was excited but
didn't know if he would be much use.
Yet look at him here, leading the early
church, bravely standing up to tell the
truth. The Holy Spirit changed Peter to
a strong, confident person ready to
stand up for Jesus. Peter said the Holy
Spirit was God's promised gift to
everyone. That means us!

Dear God, thank you that
your Holy Spirit is with us.
Help us to understand more
about him.

5 Spending their time

Peter told them many other things as well. Then he said, "I beg you to save yourselves from what will happen to all these evil people." On that day about 3000 believed his message and were baptised. They spent their time learning from the apostles, and they were like family to each other. They also broke bread and prayed together.

Acts 2:40-42

Sometimes the church is called a family. The people in the early church found it exciting to be in this family. They spent a lot of time together learning about Jesus, praying, sharing meals and other belongings. Some things are different for us now. Many of us live in big cities and our church isn't close to where we live. Some of us are in small churches, some in very big ones. Whatever it's like, belonging to church is so much more than going into a building. It is sharing our lives with other Christians, treating them as brothers and sisters. If you don't think this has happened much to you at your church, maybe it's up to you to make a start.

Dear God, help us to think of others in your church as part of your family, to spend time with them and treat them with love.

You give hope

Spring

I *n most places Spring means growth. Plants take a rest in the colder months and then begin to grow vigorously as the days get warmer. Today most produce can be bought in the sho[ps] all year round; by flying in fruit and vegetables we can always ge[t] what we want. When the Bible w[as] written, seedtime and harvest we[re] very important. If a crop failed, you needed to wait another year before trying again. The tribes who lived around God's people had special gods for every seaso[n.] God's special people trusted in th[e] one true God to meet their needs.*

Spring

 You give hope

 Our God, you deserve praise in Zion, where we keep our promises to you. Everyone will come to you because you answer prayer. Our terrible sins get us down, but you forgive us. You bless your chosen ones, and you invite them to live near you in your temple. We will enjoy your house, the sacred temple.

Psalm 65:1-4

King David knew that the most important thing was not whether the crops would grow but whether the people were sorry for what they had done wrong. How could God bless his people if they were disobedient? King David knew that sometimes God didn't answer prayers because of disobedience. The people went to their special place to pray. The temple was the place where everyone could celebrate God's help to them. But if they went not intending to change their ways and be obedient to God, he would be very sad. Saying sorry to God is something we should all do, as well as saying sorry to each other. Why not try it this weekend.

Our God, you save us, and your fearsome deeds answer our prayers for justice! You give hope to people everywhere on earth, even those across the sea. You are strong, and your mighty power put the mountains in place.

Psalm 65:5-6

God is strong. You might know a song about God being strong and mighty. You could sing it. King David knew that everyone in the world depended on God to send the rain and make the crops grow. Even people who didn't know anything about God still needed his help. If God put those great mountains in place, then surely he could help his special people. King David also knew that God wanted his world to be a fair and 'just' place. That means everyone having their fair share of food and being cared for. Perhaps you know of people who don't get their fair share of food? Perhaps you could help them this week in some way. Save a little money to give to people who are helping others would be one way.

 Father God, thank you that you are so strong. Thank you for caring about everyone in the world. Please help us to be caring as well.

2 Let's celebrate

You silence the roaring waves and the noisy shouts of the nations. People far away marvel at your fearsome deeds, and all who live under the sun celebrate and sing because of you.

Psalm 65:7-8

What a lovely picture! Everyone in the world celebrating and singing thank you songs to God. It sounds like a great big party. King David really wanted the world to be like this. He knew about wars and famines, earthquakes and floods. He also knew that people could be forgiven for doing wrong things and could treat each other justly. We have read about that already. Do you know a special 'thank you' song you could sing to God? Make a list of the things you want to say thank you for and include them in this prayer. It may be special things for you or just thank you for the world around you.

Dear God, we want to thank you for .... Help us to be happy because of all the good things you do for us. Help us to help others so they can join in with saying thank you as well.

3 Showers of rain

You take care of the earth, and send rain to help the soil grow all kinds of crops. Your rivers never run dry, and you prepare the earth to produce much grain. You water all of its fields and level the uneven ground. You send showers of rain to soften the soil and help the plants sprout.

Psalm 65:9-10

Sometimes parts of our country suffer from drought. It means no rain falls – the crops fail, animals die and the rivers dry up. It is a very sad time for the farmers. Some droughts go on a long time. However, suddenly it rains again. The brown soil turns green as the plants begin to grow. The cattle get fatter and the birds build their nests and lay their eggs. We don't know what causes the drought. Maybe it is because people have upset God's creation. Pollution and failing to look after our world has meant a lot of problems. God still wants to take care of the earth. He has made us his helpers. He wants us to be careful and treat his world with care. Talk about ways you could help to look after your environment.

Heavenly Father, thank you for sending rain so that crops will grow. Help us to take care of your world so that everyone can benefit from it.

Valleys overflow

Tell everyone

Wherever your footsteps touch the earth, rich harvest is gathered. Desert pastures blossom and mountains celebrate. Meadows are filled with sheep and goats; valleys overflow with grain and echo with joyful songs.

Psalm 65:11-13

King David finishes his poem about God's goodness by talking about the harvest. After God sends the rain the farmers plough the fields, sow the seed and care for it until the harvest. No wonder everyone sings a joyful song when the harvest is gathered in. It means everyone can eat. Bread can be baked, fruit shared around and some stored away for later. No wonder the farmers have a party. But none of this would have been possible if God had not sent the rain and put that special 'life force' in each tiny seed. In the end, everyone in the world depends on God. Without the miracle of life, all the earth would be a desert like the planets around us.

Thank you, God, for the miracle of life that we see in a tiny seed as it sprouts and babies as they grow. Thank you for being a good God who has given us so many good things.

Tell everyone on this earth to shout praises to God! Sing about his glorious name. Honour him with praises. Say to God, "Everything you do is fearsome and your mighty power makes your enemies come crawling. You are worshipped by everyone! We all sing praises to you."

Psalm 66:1-4

What shall we do for this great God who does such good things for us? Why, tell everyone about him of course! Do you know of some people, perhaps friends from church, who are telling people about God? It would be wonderful if everyone would listen and then shout praises to God. Sadly, some people don't want to know. Some people even say God isn't there at all. Telling people about God can be hard and discouraging work. We can't all go to different places to tell people about God, but we can tell our friends. We can pray for people who have gone to tell others about God and support them. Pray for them now.

Dear Father God, thank you for missionaries and pastors who tell people about you. Please help .... Keep them safe and help people listen to what they say.

19 When sad things happen

S ometimes sad things happen. When they do we want to cry and often can't sleep because we keep thinking about those sad things. When that happens, isn't it good to be able to tell someone else how we feel. Someone who understands and loves us enough to be with us even though we are sad. It doesn't help to pretend we are not sad when we are. The Psalm we will read this week is an honest poem. King David loved God and because he was very sad he knew that God would listen to him even if the reason for his sadness made him angry some of the time. David was honest with God – that's exactly what God wants.

 I pray to you, Lord God, and I beg you to listen. In days filled with trouble, I search for you. And at night I tirelessly lift my hands in prayer, refusing comfort. When I think of you, I feel restless and weak.

Psalm 77:1-3

There are all sorts of reasons why we feel sad. Sometimes it's because someone we love has died or gone away. Sometimes it's because other things change – we have to move house or school. Perhaps something we tried very hard to do didn't work or friends just let us down. King David knew about this when he wrote this Psalm but he also knew that God heard him. Why not spend some time making up a special prayer to tell God why you are sad. You might want to draw a picture of what caused you to be sad and write on it 'God hear me'. This will remind you all week that God does understand. Your prayer could begin 'Dear God, we are sad because ...'

 Dear God, we are sad because

....

I can't sleep

Because of you, Lord God, I can't sleep. I am restless and can't even talk. I think of times gone by, of those years long ago. Each night my mind is flooded with questions. "Have you rejected me for ever? Won't you be kind again? Is this the end of your love and your promises?"

Psalm 77:4-8

Poor King David – even when he went to bed he couldn't forget how sad he was. He tossed and turned but couldn't get rid of his sadness. It's dreadful when we can't sleep. The night seems very long and the house is very quiet. When David couldn't sleep, he asked God questions: 'Will you keep your promises?' 'Do you still love me?'
Of course God keeps his promises and that is what we need to remember when we are sad and can't sleep. God goes on loving us all the time. Jesus said 'I am with you always.' Jesus understands and so we can trust him to be with us, to hear us and to remind us of his promises. We aren't alone – Jesus loves us.

Dear Lord Jesus, at the moment we are very sad because .... We can't sleep very well. Please help us by being with us and giving us your special peace.

I will remember

"Have your forgotten how to have pity? Do you refuse to show mercy because of your anger?" Then I said, "God Most High, what hurts me most is that you no longer help us with your mighty arm." Our Lord, I will remember the things you have done, your miracles of long ago.

Psalm 77: 9-11

King David was even more sad and depressed. He wondered if God really did care. 'Supposing God can't help me,' he thinks. 'Supposing he isn't powerful enough.' Then God reminded David of just one thing – 'Remember – remember all the ways I helped you in the past.' When we are very sad it is good to remember. Remember the good things God has helped us with and good things that happened before the sad event. Let's remember why we are sad and tell each other some good things or happy memories about that person or thing. Remembering the happy things helps us when we are sad and telling others about those good things is even more helpful. Sharing each others' stories helps us see things God's way. He really does know everything and understands why we are sad.

Loving Heavenly Father, thank you for all our good memories. Help us with our sadness today.

3 I will think about you

*I will think about each one of
your mighty deeds. Everything
you do is right, and no other god
compares with you. You alone
work miracles, and you have let
nations see your mighty power.
With your own arm you rescued
your people, the descendants of
Jacob and Joseph.*

Psalm 77:12-15

King David began to think about the
great stories he knew, how God had
looked after his special people. He
remembered how God had helped
Jacob and Joseph. God provided a
way for his special people to have food
when everywhere else people were
starving. Even in that story, God
changed sad things into good things!
David began to realise that God understood him. If he had looked after him
so far in his life, wouldn't he keep on
looking after him? Of course he would.
David thought some more. He remembered when God had given him the
strength to defeat very powerful armies.
Of course God cared enough to look
after him! Thinking about God, who he
is and how he helps us, was good for
David long ago; it is also good for us
today. When we begin to think about
God (the Bible calls that meditating),
then everything else is easier to understand.

Dear God, help us to think
about you today. Thank you
for everything you have done
for us. Help us to trust you
today.

4 You made everything

*The ocean looked at you, God,
and it trembled deep down with
fear. Water flowed from the
clouds. Thunder was heard
above as your arrows of lightning
flashed about. Your thunder
roared like chariot wheels.
The world was made bright by
lightning, and all the earth
trembled.*

Psalm 77:16-18

Can you remember watching a great
thunderstorm? Wasn't it awesome –
the noise of the thunder and the rain
drumming on the roof and drowning
out all other sounds. At night the
lightning flashes are so bright everything around looks huge. Sometimes it
feels as if everything is shaking when
the thunder comes. David was probably
watching a storm as he wrote this
Psalm. He remembered that everything
in the world is God's creation and even
thunderstorms point back to God.
God is in control. At times, it's hard to
understand but it's true. So whatever is
making us feel sad this week, God does
understand. All creation is his. There is
nothing that he doesn't understand so
we need not be afraid.

Lord God, sometimes we feel
like David in the thunderstorm
– very afraid. But you are a
great God, you love us, so
give us the strength to watch
the storm pass and the sun
come out again.

You guided your people

You walked through the water of the mighty sea, but your footprints were never seen. You guided your people like a flock of sheep, and you chose Moses and Aaron to be their leaders.

Psalm 77:19-20

King David reaches the end of his Psalm. He began by telling God how sad he was. Then he remembered all the good things God had done. Now he has a picture of God in his mind. He thinks about God walking in front of his special people. They couldn't see him but he was there. They couldn't see his footprints but they knew what he had done. He had rescued them from the Egyptian army. He had helped them cross the Red Sea and travel through the desert. He was just like a shepherd caring for them. That was David's picture of God quite often – a loving shepherd. David wrote about God being his shepherd; can you think why? Yes, David had been a shepherd when he was a boy. God is like a shepherd for us today. He will care for us and even if times are sad and difficult he will be with us. How do we know? Because he promised and he always keeps his word.

The Lord is my shepherd – he will always be with me. Thank you Jesus for your promise. Help us to remember it and believe it today.

Merry-go-round the Bible

Bible heroes - Abraham 20

*W*hat jobs do we keep putting off? Ones we don't want to do like vacuuming, repairing the dripping tap, tidying up our bedroom or doing our homework. Getting started is usually the hardest part. Then things either go smoothly and the job's done in no time or something goes wrong and the job takes longer to finish. God wanted to use a man named Abraham to start a job for him. Abraham loved and worshipped God. When Abraham lived, a long time ago, many people were idolaters. Idolaters are people who believe in other gods. These other gods include nature, fire, the sun, the rain or people, such as a king or powerful person. To make the gods more real, people made statues and carvings and then worshipped the statue or carving. Abraham's job was to start God's plan of bringing idol worshipping people back to the true God. It was a job that took thousands of years to complete.

Abram and Sarai

God chooses Abram

After Terah was 70 years old, he had three sons: Abram, Nahor and Haran, who became the father of Lot. Terah's sons were born in the city of Ur in Chaldea, and Haran died there before the death of his father. The following is the story of Terah's descendants. Abram married Sarai, but she was not able to have any children... Terah decided to move from Ur to the land of Canaan. He took along Abram and Sarai and his grandson Lot, the son of Haran. But when they came to the city of Haran, they decided to settle there instead.

Genesis 11:26-29, 31

This is a story of a great hero of the Bible, Abram, who was later called Abraham. It begins with Abram's father who decides to take his family and move to Canaan. We aren't told why he did this, though we soon see that it was part of God's plan. However, Terah never got to Canaan. Instead he stopped about half way, in a city called Haran. Abram would have met people from many lands as he followed the trade route from Ur (in present day Iraq). He would have heard stories about different gods and how people worshipped them. But Abram seems to have known about the one true God. And the one true God had a very special plan for Abram. Abram was called to leave where he was and go to a strange land to serve God. Who do we know who has done that today? Who has read about them in a magazine or heard them speak in church? Let's pray a special prayer asking God to be with them and protect them today.

The Lord said to Abram: "Leave your country, your family and your relatives and go to the land that I will show you. I will bless you and make your descendants into a great nation. You will become famous and be a blessing to others. I will bless anyone who blesses you, but I will put a curse on anyone who puts a curse on you. Everyone on earth will be blessed because of you."

Genesis 12:1-3

Have you ever been class captain, a school councillor or won a special award? What special job did you get picked for at school, work or home? How did you feel? Abram was a person who kept worshipping the true God at a time when people had other gods. Even Terah, Abram's father, worshipped other gods. Perhaps that is why God told Abram to leave his father's home, relatives and country. God chose Abram to do a special job for him. God chose Abram to have many descendants. Do you know what a descendant is? Abram's descendants will become an important and famous nation. God will bless them so that others will be blessed and made happy.

Dear Lord, help us to follow and love you even when people around us follow their own ways. Help us to live the way you want.

2 God's promise

3 Abram believed

The Lord said to Abram: "Look around to the north, south, east, and west. I will give you and your family all the land you can see. It will be theirs for ever! I will give you more descendants than there are specks of dust on the earth, and some day it will be easier to count the specks of dust than to count your descendants. Now walk backwards and forwards across the land, because I am giving it to you."

Genesis 13:14b-17

What sort of promises do we have to keep? Do people in our family get pocket money if they do certain jobs? Do we make promises to others? Are they easy to keep? In these verses, God makes a promise to Abram. He said he would give Abram two things. What were they? Notice how much land and how many descendants Abram was to receive. Remember God said that Abram would have these so others would be blessed. Notice God says, 'I will give you ...'. There is no 'if' for Abram to keep. Perhaps Abram had already done his part when he believed in God when other people were turning away from him. What does God say he will give Abram?

Thank you Lord for the promises in the Bible. Thank you that you will always love and care for us.

Later the Lord spoke to Abram in a vision, "Abram, don't be afraid! I will protect you and reward you greatly." But Abram answered, "Lord All-Powerful, you have given me everything I could ask for, except children. And when I die, Eliezer of Damascus will get all I own. You have not given me any children, and this servant of mine will inherit everything." The Lord replied, "No, he won't! You will have a son of your own, and everything you have will be his." Then the Lord took Abram outside and said, "Look at the sky and see if you can count the stars. That's how many descendants you will have." Abram believed the Lord, and the Lord was pleased with him.

Genesis 15:1-6

Have you ever tried to count the stars in the sky? There are so many it would be impossible! God gave Abram the picture of the stars in the sky to remind him that he would have an uncount-able number of descendants. Abram was 86 years old and began to wonder when his wife Sarai would have their first child and start this long line of descendants. Abram had adopted Eliezer, one of his slaves, to be his heir as was the custom then. But God said that Abram's own son would be his first descendant.

Heavenly Father, when things don't seem to be going right, help us to keep on trusting in you.

Promise repeated

 # Promise kept

 Abram was 99 years old when the Lord appeared to him again and said, "I am God All-Powerful. If you obey me and always do right, I will keep my solemn promise to you and give you more descendants than can be counted." Abram bowed with his face to the ground, and God said: "I promise that you will be the father of many nations. That's why I now change your name from Abram to Abraham."

Genesis 17:1-5

'How many times have I told you?' Do we hear that in our house? Sometimes we have to be reminded over and over to do something. Is there a special event coming up? Have you forgotten? Here we read for the third time of God's promise to Abram. Abram was 99 and Sarai 89 years old. It seemed impossible that they could still have a baby. But Abram is reminded that God is all powerful. He is also reminded to do always what is right and to keep following God. What does Abram do when God reminds him of his promise? As an encouragement to Abram, God changes his name to Abraham which means 'father of many nations'.

 Thank you Lord that you always keep your promises. Help us to remember what you have promised and obey you.

 The Lord was good to Sarah and kept his promise. Although Abraham was very old, Sarah had a son exactly at the time God had said. Abraham named his son Isaac, and when the boy was eight days old, Abraham circumcised him, just as the Lord had commanded. Abraham was 100 years old when Isaac was born, and Sarah said, "God has made me laugh. Now everyone will laugh with me."

Genesis 21:1-6

It's Christmas at last! For months there's been advertisements on TV. We've made lists of things we want, bought food, wrapped presents and counted the days down. Who's wondering if they'll get the present they want. It's hard waiting for an exciting time. At last Sarah is pregnant and has a son. How did Sarah feel about her new son? Isaac was born in God's time and his name Isaac meant laughter. So many generations followed with many, many descendants. One of the descendants many thousands of years later was Jesus. We can read the very long list in Luke chapter 3 starting at verse 23.

 Thank God for a promise he has kept for you.

21

God bless you

When visitors come

Visitors to our home are very special. They tell us stories of what they have been doing since we last met. It's great fun. This week we 're reading part of a letter Paul wrote to his friends in Philippi. e really wanted to visit them but couldn't. He had been put in jail o he wrote a letter instead. The Christians at Philippi were so orried about Paul being in rison that they sent him a gift help. Paul wanted to say thank ou. He also wanted to encourage the Philippians in case they found emselves in prison for the same eason. 'Stand firm without being ightened,' he said. Paul hoped at one day he would be able to sit them and encourage them.

 ## WE. God bless you

From Paul and Timothy, servants of Christ Jesus. To all of God's people who belong to Christ Jesus at Philippi and to all of your church officials and officers. I pray that God our Father and the Lord Jesus Christ will be kind to you and will bless you with peace!

Philippians 1:1-2

We know who wrote this letter and we know who was to receive it – everyone in the church at Philippi. If Paul had managed to get there himself, there would have been a lot of excitement. We get excited when we have visitors, don't we? Paul's letter starts with a prayer. He asks God to be kind to his friends and to bless them. He wants God to give them peace, which really means he wants them to live peacefully with their neighbours and their family and themselves. What sort of prayer will we make up for our visitors? We could ask God to give them a safe journey and keep them well. Don't forget to ask God to be kind to them and to bless them. Who will write it out neatly and who will give it to them when they arrive?

1 I thank my God

Every time I think of you, I thank my God. And whenever I mention you in my prayers, it makes me happy. This is because you have taken part with me in spreading the good news from the first day you heard about it. God is the one who began this good work in you and I am certain that he won't stop before it is complete on the day that Christ Jesus returns.

Philippians 1:3-6

Paul really liked his friends in the church at Philippi. He tells us it made him happy to pray for them. He remembered how they helped him tell people about Jesus. I expect he pictured them in his mind when he was praying. We can do that or even look at a photo of the person we are praying for. Praying for other people is one way of sharing with them in the things they do. Perhaps we could make a list of people we want to pray for and pin it up to remind us. We can include our visitors and family members who don't live in our home and people who work telling others about Jesus. Can we think of some from our church or other family friends? Don't forget to add our names to the list.

Dear Lord Jesus, thank you for our family and friends. Please be kind to them and look after them today.

2 You have a special place

You have a special place in my heart. So it is only natural for me to feel the way I do. All of you have helped in the work that God has given me, as I defend the good news and tell about it here in jail. God himself knows how much I want to see you. He knows that I care for you in the same way that Christ Jesus does.

Philippians 1:7-8

Poor Paul – he really wanted to go to see his friends. Sadly he was stuck in jail. He hadn't done anything wrong – he just told people about Jesus. Some people didn't like that because they wanted to continue with their selfish lives. In some countries many Christians are put in jail because they follow Jesus. But Paul wasn't put off by being in jail; he just told the prisoners and the warders about Jesus. Do you know of any countries where Christians are persecuted or put in jail? They would love to visit their friends or even just run on the grass and feel the sunshine. Thank God that we are able to be followers of Jesus without ending up in prison. Pray for people who are in prison just because they love Jesus.

Dear God, please help people who are in jail just because they are Christians. Be very near to them and give them courage.

Right choices

*I pray that your love will keep
on growing and that you will fully
know and understand how to
make the right choices. Then you
will still be pure and innocent
when Christ returns. And until
that day, Jesus Christ will keep
you busy doing good deeds that
bring glory and praise to God.*

Philippians 1:9-10

Making right choices can be very
difficult. How many choices have you
already made today? Which ones were
easy? Choosing to get up? What were
more difficult? Choosing to say sorry?
Making right choices means understanding the alternatives. If we stay in
bed we might get into trouble at school
or at work. Jesus wants us to choose to
do good things. He wants us to do the
things that please God our Heavenly
Father. What could we choose to do
today that would please God? What
about keeping a list so that later we
can look back to see if we managed
to make the right choices.

Dear Lord Jesus, show us the
things we ought to do that will
please you. Help us to be
obedient to your rules.

Consider others

*Christ encourages you, and his
love comforts you. God's Spirit
unites you, and you are concerned
for others. Now make me completely happy! Live in harmony
by showing love for each other.
Be united in what you think,
as if you were only one person.
Don't be jealous or proud, but be
humble and consider others more
important than yourselves. Care
about them as much as you care
about yourselves.*

Philippians 2:1-4

It's easy to get jealous. We think when
someone else gets top marks or drives
around in a new car, 'Wish it were me.'
Paul knew that jealous people stop
caring for each other. Jealousy destroys
friendships because it's all about 'me'.
God wants us to care for other people
just as if they were us. Then we won't
be jealous of them, we will be pleased
for them. When someone does something special we should give them a pat
on the back and say 'Well done.' That's
called encouragement. Jesus encourages us by helping us see how important we are to him. We should treat
others the same way. If you have
special visitors this week, encourage
them and see how pleased they will be.

Heavenly Father, help me to
be an encouragement today.
Help me encourage someone
else and keep me from being
jealous.

Jesus is Lord

Christ was truly God.
But he did not try to remain equal
with God.
He gave up everything and became
a slave,
when he became like one of us.

Christ was humble.
He obeyed God
and even died on a cross.
Then God gave Christ the
highest place
and honoured his name above
all others.

So at the name of Jesus
everyone will bow down,
those in heaven, on earth,
and under the earth.
And to the glory of God the Father
everyone will openly agree,
"Jesus Christ is Lord!"

Philippians 2:6-11

This special poem is a picture of Jesus.
It tells us what he did for us and then
what God his father did for him. Paul
wants his friends to be like Jesus. This
is very hard but God put the Spirit of
Jesus in us to help us. Jesus gave up
everything to help us – he wasn't
jealous or boastful. He was humble and
obedient. That's a great challenge for
everyone.

Lord Jesus, help us to be
more like you today so that
others will know we love you
and obey you.

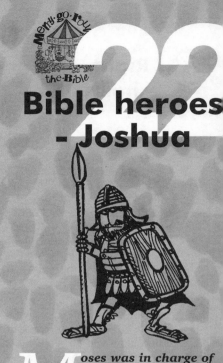

Bible heroes - Joshua

Moses was in charge of
leading God's people, th
Israelites, on the journe
to the Promised Land o
Canaan. After crossing the Red
Sea, the Israelites spent about
forty years wandering from place
to place in the desert. They often
complained and grumbled becaus
life was difficult. But God looked
after them and kept his promise
even though it seemed to take a
long time. Like Moses, Joshua
loved God and followed his ways.
Moses had trained Joshua to take
over the job of leading the Israelites.

Joshua was obedient when he was
a young man. He had reminded
the people that God kept his word
But the people did not believe him
So for forty years Joshua acted as
a helper to Moses. In that time, he
became a wise leader and ruler so
that he was ready to take over
when Moses died.

WE. A disobedient people

1 God with Joshua

Moses and Aaron bowed down to pray in front of the crowd. Joshua and Caleb tore their clothes in sorrow and said, "We saw the land ourselves and it's very good. If we obey the Lord, he will surely give us that land rich with milk and honey. So don't rebel. We have no reason to be afraid of the people who live there. The Lord is on our side, and they won't stand a chance against us!"

Numbers 14:5-9

When did we last go and stay at a different place? It's fun looking in rooms, opening cupboards and drawers and exploring outside. Joshua and Caleb were two of twelve men who were sent to Canaan to discover how many people lived there. How strong were they? Did they live in towns or cities with walls round them? Was the land fertile or poor? After forty days of exploring, they returned and reported to Moses that the land was rich and fertile. But the Canaanites were big and powerful and lived in large cities with big walls. The Israelites were discouraged and whinged and complained. 'It would have been better to die in Egypt than come here. How can we take over? Let's choose another leader to go back to Egypt.' They had forgotten God was with them. Their job was to trust and follow him. Joshua and Caleb reminded them that God was with them and he would protect them. They must not be afraid. Sadly they refused to believe and God left them to wander in the desert for another 40 years.

Moses, the Lord's servant, was dead. So the Lord spoke to Joshua son of Nun, who had been the assistant of Moses. The Lord said: "My servant Moses is dead. Now you must lead Israel across the Jordan River into the land I am giving to all of you. Wherever you go, I will give you that land, as I promised Moses. It will reach from the Southern Desert to the Lebanon mountains in the north, and to the north-east as far as the great Euphrates River. It will include the land of the Hittites, and the land from here at the Jordan River to the Mediterranean Sea on the west. Joshua, I will always be with you and help you as I helped Moses, and no one will ever be able to defeat you."

Joshua 1:1-5

It often takes a long time for a new leader to take over a group. This was the case for Joshua. He was Moses' personal assistant for many years, chosen to be the person to take over from Moses when he died. Moses had seen the Promised Land from a distance but Joshua would take the people to live there. God now speaks to Joshua. What does God tell him? This is a wonderful start for Joshua as leader. He knows that God will be with him and care for him.

 Thank you God that you promise to be with us. Help us to know that you are with us all the time.

Be strong and brave

 ## Crossing the Jordan

"Long ago I promised the ancestors of Israel that I would give this land to their descendants. So be strong and brave! Be careful to do everything my servant Moses taught you. Never stop reading 'The Book of the Law' he gave you. Day and night you must think about what it says. If you obey it completely, you and Israel will be able to take this land. I have commanded you to be strong and brave. Don't ever be afraid or discouraged! I am the Lord your God and I will be there to help you wherever you go."

Joshua 1:6-9

How do you feel when you have to speak in front of a group? Think of when you have to give news, a speech or a report to the class or at work. How confident you feel depends how well prepared you are. God commands Joshua to be strong and brave as leader of the Israelites. Joshua is not an outlaw or a robber about to take over other people's property. He is a servant carrying out the directions of the Lord God. He has strict instructions as to what he must do each day. He was to be confident that God would be with him wherever he went. He obeyed God and God kept his promises.

 Thank you, Lord for your word the Bible. Help us to learn to do what it says.

Joshua chose twelve men; he called them together, and told them: "Go into the middle of the riverbed where the sacred chest is, and pick up a large rock. Carry it on your shoulder to our camp. There are twelve of you, so there will be one rock for each tribe. Some day your children will ask, 'Why are these rocks here?' Then you can tell them how the water stopped flowing when the chest was being carried across the river. These rocks will always remind our people of what happened here today."

Joshua 4:4-7

Do you have a keepsake of something special in your life – the hospital band from your wrist when you were a baby or something you brought back from a holiday? Trophies, certificates or degrees remind us of significant times. The Israelites were moving again to Canaan. They had to cross the Jordan River and this time there wasn't any questioning. God had taken them through the Red Sea, he could take them across the river. When all the people and animals had crossed over, Joshua sent twelve men back to collect one large stone each from the middle. What were they for?

 Dear God, thank you for the reminders we have of the good times in our life. Help us to remember that you always love us.

The walls fell down

 On the seventh day, the army got up at daybreak. They marched slowly around Jericho the same as they had done for the past six days, except on this day they went around seven times. Then the priests blew the trumpets, and Joshua yelled: "Get ready to shout! The Lord will let you capture this town ..." The priests blew their trumpets again, and the soldiers shouted as loud as they could. The walls of Jericho fell flat. Then the soldiers rushed up the hill, went straight into the town, and captured it.

Joshua 6:15-16 and 20

Who has experienced an earth tremor, or a bad storm with strong winds and beating rain? Both can leave a lot of damage with cracks in the walls, fallen trees and powerlines. Here, another big event was about to happen in the Israelites' journey. God was going to give them the city of Jericho, a city surrounded by a high strong wall. Joshua, his soldiers and the priests marched around the outside of the city wall once a day for six days. The soldiers didn't make a sound but the priests blew their trumpets. What was different on the seventh day? What was the result of all this noise? Imagine how surprised the people of Jericho would have been.

 Lord, you are such a powerful God. Help us to trust in you in everything we do.

A faithful follower

 The Lord let Israel live in peace with its neighbours for a long time and Joshua lived to a ripe old age. One day he called a meeting of the leaders of the tribes of Israel, including the old men, the judges, and the officials. Then he told them: "I am now very old. You have seen how the Lord your God fought for you and helped you defeat the nations who lived in this land ... Be sure that you carefully obey everything written in 'The Book of the Law' of Moses and do exactly what it says."

Joshua 23:1-3 and 6

Have you an older friend who gives you advice? How do you decide if it is good or bad advice? At last the Israelites were in the Promised Land of Canaan. Joshua divided up the land. He gave some to each of the twelve tribes. The Lord had given the Israelites security from their enemies. How do you think Joshua felt knowing that? Joshua is now old and gives a farewell speech to the elders of the people. He reminds the people of what God has done for them and tells them that they must continue to follow God and live in his ways. Why was this good advice?

 Heavenly Father, thank you for the people who teach us to live your ways. Help them to give good advice.

Bible heroes - Isaiah

I saiah lived 700 years or so before Jesus. He was a prophet. This means that he was chosen by God to listen to him and then to tell others what God had to say to them.

Isaiah lived in Jerusalem and he was probably a prince. He would have been well educated. Many of his prophecies are recorded and have been collected together in the Bible. Poor Isaiah had a difficult time. His job was to persuade people to listen to God or they would be punished. That is exactly what happened. However, Isaiah was also given a vision of what God would do in the future. In particular, he prophesied that God was concerned about people from every nation and that God loved them and would help them learn to be his followers as well. Isaiah watched while many foreign armies invaded the land. But he never forgot that God had called him to speak out for him.

WE.

The Lord said: "I will sing a song about my friend's vineyard that was on the side of a fertile hill. My friend dug the ground, removed the stones, and planted the best vines. He built a watch-tower and dug a pit in rocky ground for pressing the grapes. He hoped they would be sweet, but bitter grapes were all it produced. Listen, people of Jerusalem and Judah! You be the judge of me and my vineyard. What more could I have done for my vineyard? I hoped for sweet grapes, but bitter grapes were all that grew."

Isaiah 5:1-4

Who's doing some gardening this week? We could try some alfalfa seeds on a patch of wet cloth on a plate or some radish or sunflower seeds in a pot or in the garden. If we give our 'garden' the right kind of care we can *expect* some good results. God's message to Judah, his 'vineyard' (or garden) was that he had put a lot of work in to it to give them the best grapes, but their 'fruit' wasn't very sweet. God gives us so much. What are some things he might expect from us? God spent many years teaching his people. But they became selfish and failed to live up to his expectations. God then had to send a prophet to challenge them and call them back to himself.

Holy, holy, holy

In the year that King Uzziah died, I had a vision of the Lord. He was on his throne high above, and his robe filled the temple. Flaming creatures with six wings each were flying over him. They covered their faces with two of their wings and their bodies with two more. They used the other two wings for flying, as they shouted, "Holy, holy, holy, Lord All-Powerful! The earth is filled with your glory."

Isaiah 6:1-3

God is loving: no question about that. But that's not all he is. He never cheats, or lies, or is selfish, or loses his temper. He is good, so good that he is very very different from anyone we've ever known. One word for this is 'holy'. Somehow we have to try and grasp the fact that God is white-hot pure. That means that he can do nothing wrong at all. But God is also loving which means he will help his friends be pure and loving as well. We have a great God. Isn't it wonderful that he really loves each one of us?

Our Lord God, All-Powerful, and holy, we're sorry if we've sometimes thought of you too lightly. Help us to give you the respect that you deserve.

Forgiveness

As they shouted, the doorposts of the temple shook, and the temple was filled with smoke. Then I cried out, "I'm doomed! Everything I say is sinful, and so are the words of everyone around me. Yet I have seen the King, the Lord All-Powerful." One of the flaming creatures flew over to me with a burning coal that it had taken from the altar with a pair of metal tongs. It touched my lips with the hot coal and said, "This has touched your lips. Your sins are forgiven, and you are no longer guilty."

Isaiah 6:4-7

Isaiah felt totally out of place in the presence of a holy God. It was like he'd come in from shovelling manure in the garden, or playing in the mud, and found himself standing on a white carpet in a room all set up for a party. He didn't go for the soap, however. He knew the dirt was inside and, when God was ready for it, God would do the cleansing. Isaiah's special picture tells us the truth about God. He doesn't want us doing bad things and feeling guilty. He wants us to be sorry and forgiven.

Lord God, we know we don't deserve to be accepted by you. It's wonderful that you still want us to come near to you. Thank you that when we are ready to be forgiven, you're ready to forgive us.

3 God's messenger

4 The bad news first

Isaiah was forgiven. All the painful memory of failure and disobedience, all the dirtiness, was gone. He felt clean and free and glad in God's presence – and grateful. What could he do to show God how thankful he was?

After this, I heard the Lord ask, "Is there anyone I can send? Will someone go for us?" "I'll go," I answered. "Send me." Then the Lord told me to go and speak this message to the people: "You will listen and listen, but never understand. You will look and look, but never see."

Isaiah 6:8-9

Now he knew what he could do for God. He knew also how hard it would be to speak to people who didn't want to listen. He would go and tell the people what he knew about God. He would also tell them what God expected from them.

Lord we are thankful for your love to us, shown in so many ways. For the things you give us, for the way you take care of us, and especially for the way you keep on forgiving us, thank you. Please show us ways we can serve you. Help us to be ready to do the hard things as well as the easy ones.

Then I asked the Lord, "How long will this last?" The Lord answered: "Until their towns are destroyed and their houses are deserted, until their fields are empty, and I have sent them far away, leaving their land in ruins. If only a tenth of the people are left, even they will be destroyed. But just as stumps remain after trees have been cut down, some of my chosen ones will be left."

Isaiah 6:11-13

Isaiah did have some good news to tell. But the bad news had to come first. Most people didn't want to know anything about what God wished to tell them. What could God do? Sadly, he just had to let them be overrun by their enemies till they were almost destroyed. But not quite all. A few wanted to hear, and Isaiah was able to pass on to them the wonderful promise that what looked like the end, wouldn't be the end.

We're glad, Lord, that your love for us is a tough love, even though we find this uncomfortable at times. Thank you that you never give up on us. Thank you that even if things get very bad for us, you are there, and we can trust you.

Rescued!

Those who walked in the dark have seen a bright light. And it shines upon everyone who lives in the land of darkest shadows. Our Lord, you have made your nation stronger. Because of you, its people are glad and celebrate like workers at harvest time or like soldiers dividing what they have taken. You have broken the power of those who abused and enslaved your people. You have rescued them just as you saved your people from Midian ... A child has been born for us. We have been given a son who will be our ruler.

Isaiah 9:2-4, 6a

At last, Isaiah has some good news! Though it wasn't going to happen for 700 years, it was written into God's plan. In fact this news was so certain that Isaiah wrote about it as though it had already happened! What on earth is he talking about? – 'a bright light', a rescue? Then comes the clue: 'a child has been born for us ... who will be our ruler.' Yes, it's Jesus he's talking about. If you have time, read the Bible passage again with this in mind.

Thank you God for taking so much trouble to plan ahead for Jesus to come to earth as a baby, and grow up to be our great Rescuer. May we walk in his light and reflect it to others. "Shine, Jesus, shine, fill this land ..."

A wonderful harvest

Autumn

A s the hot summer sun begins to cool some crops get harvested. The grapes are gathered from the vines and other fruit from the trees. Autumn is a special time to remember good things that God gives to us. When times are good, it is easy to forget that it is God who cares for us. The Psalms we will read this week are special songs saying thank you to God. In Psalm 66 the writer says thank you to God for hearing his prayer. In Psalm 67 the writer wants everyone to join in saying thank you for the harvest.

WE. Don't turn against God

 Come and see the fearsome things our God has done! When God made the sea dry up, our people walked across, and because of him, we celebrated there. His mighty power rules for ever, and nothing the nations do can be hidden from him. So don't turn against God.

Psalm 66:5-7

The writer reminds people listening to this song of an unusual event when God helped his special people. Have you heard this story before? The people remembered how the Egyptians chased their ancestors and God opened up the sea and rescued them. They never forgot that and made sure that their children and their children's children knew about that. Can you remember times when God helped you or our family? (Probably everyone can think of something.) It is really great to have memories and particularly to remember when God has helped us. Remember these times this week as you read these special songs.

A land of plenty

 All of you people, come and praise our God! Let his praises be heard. God protects us from death and keeps us steady. Our God, you tested us, just as silver is tested. You trapped us in a net and gave us heavy burdens. You sent war chariots to crush our skulls. We travelled through fire and through floods, but you brought us to a land of plenty.

Psalm 66:8-12

The people keep on remembering what happened in their long journey with Moses. Warring tribes attacked them and they had to fight their enemies. They forgot God and made idols. All sorts of bad things happened. There was little water and dry hot deserts. In the end however, God brought them to a special place. He called it a 'land of plenty'. When they settled there, life became much easier. Then, the great temptation was to forget God. God's special people needed reminding that they still depended on him, even though the dreadful days of wandering in the desert were over. It is easy to forget about God when things are going well.

 Dear Father God, help us to remember you today. Help us to be obedient to you and to show that we love you.

Come and listen

I will bring sacrifices into your house, my God, and I will do what I promised when I was in trouble. I will sacrifice my best sheep and offer bulls and goats on your altar. All who worship God, come here and listen; I will tell you everything God has done for me.

Psalm 66:13-16

The best way to go on remembering God is to tell each other what he has done for us. Sometimes when we are in trouble we make silly promises. The writer of this song remembers the promises he made when he was in trouble and keeps his word. He also tells other people what God has done for him. What sort of promises have you made when you were in trouble? Sometimes they can't be kept but this writer is going to keep his word. He will sacrifice the best for God. Sometimes we give only our second best to God. We don't make time to pray and we keep for ourselves what we ought to give to God. Let's give God our very best today so that other people might know that we love him and want to worship him.

Dear God, thank you for all you have done for us. Help us to do our best for you today.

God did listen

I prayed to the Lord, and I praised him. If my thoughts had been sinful, he would have refused to hear me. But God did listen and answered my prayer. Let's praise God! He listened when I prayed, and he is always kind.

Psalm 66:17-20

God does listen. He hears our prayers and understands what we are talking about. He also knows what is best for us. That isn't always what we think we want. We can't understand God because he is so much greater than we are. Sometimes we really want God to do something and it doesn't happen. Does that mean God didn't hear us? No! It means God has a different answer to our prayer. God is always kind. We can't understand sometimes and from our point of view sad things happen. But God knows and understands. He cares about us when we are happy and he is especially close to us when we are sad. Let's praise God! He listens to us when we pray and he is always kind.

Thank you God, for listening to our prayer. We particularly want to ask you today

....

Then everyone will follow you

 ## A wonderful harvest

 Our God, be kind and bless us! Be pleased and smile. Then everyone on earth will learn to follow you, and all nations will see your power to save us. Make everyone praise you and shout your praises ... because you judge fairly and guide all nations.

Psalm 67:1-4

This is another very special prayer. It would be wonderful if everyone followed God. If only God would make everyone praise him the world would be a wonderful place. But this writer knows that God never 'makes' people do things. He wants them to praise him but he leaves it to every person to decide – to praise him and obey him or not. That's a very wonderful gift. None of us likes it when we are made to do something we don't want. Even if we are made to do the right thing, we feel sulky and sad. God doesn't want sulky, sad people to praise him. He wants people who have chosen to follow him to praise him – that's real praise.

 Thank you God for allowing us to decide to follow you. Help us to decide to praise you because we want to and we know it will please you.

 Make everyone praise you and shout your praises. Our God has blessed the earth with a wonderful harvest! Pray for his blessings to continue and for everyone on earth to worship our God.

Psalm 67:5-7

God gives a special harvest. The writer wants everyone on earth to worship God, but knows that will only happen if people choose to do so. So he asks us to pray for two things. The first is that God will go on blessing his people. God has promised to do that and so we know that he will answer that prayer. We don't know what his blessing will be but we know that God is kind. The second thing we are asked to pray for is that everyone will worship God. Sometimes God wants us to be the answer to our own prayer. Is there someone we ought to invite to church with us this week? Perhaps there is a friend we can take to Kids' Club or Sunday School. Maybe God wants us to do something rather than just pray.

 Dear Father God, please help us to know who to invite to share in our worship of you with your people.

Each day that we live

A week with a birthday

Aren't birthdays fun! The surprise parcels, the cards brought by the post man, the special party or outing, all help to make birthdays special. Sometimes grown ups pretend they don't like birthdays. But secretly everyone likes having a fuss made for them. Every birthday is special however many we have had before. Birthdays are a way of marking of the time. They are times to think about all the things that have happened since last birthday. One of the things we can remember at our birthday is how much God loves us and how he will go on loving us in the future.

The Psalm we are reading this week is a good Psalm for birthdays because it reminds us to praise God - praise him every day and particularly on special days.

 Each day we live

 With all my heart I praise the Lord , and with all that I am I praise his holy name. With all my heart I praise the Lord! I will never forget how kind he has been. The Lord forgives our sins, heals us when we are sick and protects us from death. His kindness and love are a crown on our heads. Each day that we live, he provides for our needs and gives us the strength of a young eagle.

Psalm 103:1-5

On birthdays it is good to have a special verse of the Bible to remember. The first part of verse 17 says: 'The Lord is always kind to those who worship him'. Why don't we all learn it as a special birthday verse for the birthday person. Who will write the verse out neatly on a piece of card? Who will put it on the table? Now cover up the words one at a time and all recite the words one by one. We can cover the words with counters or even coins (these could go in the birthday person's money box at the end). When we are all together during the week, we can practice reciting the verse so it becomes special for all of us.

The Lord is always kind to those who worship him

God forgives

The Lord is merciful! He is kind and patient, and his love never fails. The Lord won't always be angry and point out our sins; he doesn't punish us as our sins deserve.

Psalm 103:8-10

Isn't it wonderful to know God forgives us? He doesn't remember the bad things we have done if we are truly sorry and ask him to forgive us. God loves us so much that he sent Jesus. Jesus died on the cross and therefore God can forgive us if we are Jesus' friend. Isn't that a fantastic birthday present. We can start again. Anything we have done to spoil the year just gone can be forgiven. A new year lies ahead and a new start. But we don't have to wait for a birthday to make a new start. We can do that any time. That's why King David kept saying 'Praise the Lord'. He kept remembering the times God had forgiven him. David was always making up songs about God – he danced and clapped for joy when he thought about God. This is a special week. Is anyone going to dance and clap for joy? Whenever we feel like this, let's 'Praise the Lord' for the new beginning he gives us every day.

Oh God, help me to praise you and not forget you when I am excited about other things. Thank you for forgiving me and giving me a new start.

God's love is great

How great is God's love for all who worship him? Greater than the distance between heaven and earth! How far has the Lord taken our sins from us? Further than the distance from east to west!

Psalm 103:11-12

Wow! How great God must be – higher than the sky! Millions and millions of kilometres. How far is the east from the west? Have a think. Imagine the world as an orange or an apple. If you put your finger on it and pretend to go east you end up where you started. If you pretend to go west the same thing happens. King David wasn't really describing God exactly. He just wanted people to know that God's love is bigger than anything we could ever imagine. When he promised to forgive us that's exactly what he will do. All those wrong things that we have told him we are sorry about are now so far away they will never be found again. No wonder King David kept on saying 'Praise the Lord'. Perhaps when he got to this bit he even did a little dance for joy. Don't you feel so happy to know that such a great God loves you?

Thank you dear God for all your love. Thank you that you always keep your promises. Help us all today to remember you. Praise the Lord!

The Lord is King

... to those who worship him

Just as parents are kind to their children, the Lord is kind to all who worship him, because he knows we are made of dust. We humans are like grass or wild flowers that quickly bloom. But a scorching wind blows, and they quickly wither to be for ever forgotten.

Psalm 103:13-16

King David had quite a lot of children and he knew that he had to be kind to them. I expect he also remembered times when he hadn't been very kind at all and had made lots of mistakes. But he also remembered that God wasn't like him and didn't make mistakes. He was always kind, though he does expect us to obey him. David knew that we can be very weak sometimes. The world can seem very big and frightening. Yet God knows all about that because he made us. He gave us our life and he watches over us all. That's encouraging isn't it? We don't know what will happen in the future but we do know that whatever happens, God will be kind to us. King David remembered that and so can we. Praise the Lord.

Dear Heavenly Father, thank you for promising to be kind to us even when we feel very small and weak. Thank you that you understand.

The Lord is always kind to those who worship him, and he keeps his promises to their descendants who faithfully obey him. God has set up his kingdom in heaven and he rules the whole creation.

Psalm 103:17-19

'The Lord is always kind to those who worship him.' All who are his friends like to talk to him and want him to help them. How many generations are there in your family? How far can you count back? One generation to Mum and Dad, another to grandparents, another to great grandparents. Some people can trace their generations back many, many years. God's love and goodness lasts all those generations, in fact, for ever. King David had a palace with a throne in it. He often sat on his throne and made decisions about what should be done. King David pictured God on a throne in heaven. He saw God's love could last for ever. David knew that he wouldn't last for ever. He would die and another generation would follow him. But God is different to that – he is a king whose love lasts for ever.

Loving father, thank you that whatever happens, your love is for ever. Praise the Lord.

Come and praise

All of you mighty angels, who obey God's commands, come and praise your Lord! All of you thousands who serve and obey God, come and praise your Lord! All of God's creation and all that he rules, come and praise your Lord! With all my heart I praise the Lord!

Psalm 103:20-22

Has it been a good week for us? Did the birthday go well? King David seems to have had a good time writing this special Psalm. He was so excited by God's love that he almost didn't know how to finish the song. King David thought about the angels in heaven. How exciting to experience God's love all day and every day.   The special angels probably also praised the Lord as they went about doing what God asked them. King David hoped that everyone would honour God as king and praise him every day. Of course we know that there are lots of people in the world who know nothing about God. They don't praise him every day. And there are other people who pretend he isn't there. They don't praise him every day. But *we* know God. We know he loves us and we can praise him and say thank you to him. That's what God expects.

Thank you Lord God that you are so kind and you love us so much. Help us to praise you today and every day.

Bible heroes - Daniel

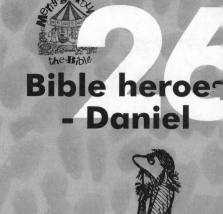

*T*he Babylonians invaded Judah, and dragged away many of the people to their own country to be their slaves. The Babylonians were an ancient race of people who had built great cities and cultures. Their great warrior king Nebuchadnezzar captured many countries and cities. On one raid, he took some hostages from Judah. The hostages were to make sure that Judah paid taxes to Babylon. One of the hostages was Daniel. He was a very clever young man and soon he began to be educated by the Babylonians. They Babylonians wrote many important books about medicine, botany, zoology and mathematics amongst others. Daniel was in the right place to learn a lot but he already knew the most important thing. God is the God of the whole world and only he is to be worshipped.

Daniel honoured

 One day the king ordered Ashpenaz, his highest palace official, to choose some young men from the royal family of Judah and from other leading Jewish families. The king said, "They must be healthy, handsome, smart, wise, educated and fit to serve in the royal palace. Teach them how to speak and write our language ... Train them for three years, and then they can become court officials." Four of the young Jews chosen were Daniel, Hananiah, Mishael, and Azariah.

Daniel 1:3-6

We feel great, don't we, when the coach puts us on the team! Daniel and his friends were chosen to be trained to look after the new king. It meant they had to work hard and learn lots. God offers us a place on his team. He knows how special each one of us is. This week think about what it means to be on God's team.

While we are together, let's all write a list of the things we do well. Let's help each other to do this. At the bottom of each page, write: 'Thank you God for making me special.' Read out all the lists.

 Some years later, King Nebuchadnezzar had a horrible nightmare – and then couldn't remember what it was about! He got very angry when none of his wise men could enlighten him. Daniel prayed, hard. God made him able to tell the king what the dream was, and what it meant.

The king said, "Now I know that your God is above all other gods and kings, because he gave you the power to explain this mystery." The king then presented Daniel with a lot of gifts; he promoted him to governor of Babylon Province and put him in charge of the other wise men.

Daniel 2:47-48

Newsflash: DANIEL TELLS KING'S DREAM – PROMOTED

If there were newspapers or TV in Daniel's day, he would have made the headlines many times. He trusted God and did his job well, and became important even though he was a foreigner in Babylon. Despite this, he was never afraid to tell people that he trusted God.

 Help us to remember that you are more important and powerful than anyone on earth, Lord.

2 Honest and faithful

3 Daniel's prayer

 Many years later, there was a new king called Darius, and Daniel became his servant too.

Darius divided his kingdom into 120 states and placed a governor in charge of each one. In order to make sure that his government was run properly, Darius put three other officials in charge of the governors. One of these officials was Daniel. And he did his work so much better than the other governors and officials that the king decided to let him govern the whole kingdom. The other men tried to find something wrong with the way Daniel did his work for the king. But they could not accuse him of anything wrong, because he was honest and faithful and did everything he was supposed to do.

Daniel 6:1-4

Newsflash: KING'S FAVOURITE REWARDED – RUMOURS OF PLOT

Daniel did nothing wrong. But others became jealous, and tried to pull him down. What nasty things have been said about you or a friend, unfairly, perhaps when you've done well? Daniel just kept on doing his job, and talking to God.

 It's hard to be like Daniel, Lord, when others are knocking us. Help us to keep our cool and concentrate on what you think of us.

 They all went to the king and said: "Your Majesty, we hope you live for ever! All your officials, leaders, advisers and governors agree that you should make a law forbidding anyone to pray to any god or human except you for the next 30 days. Everyone who disobeys this law must be thrown into a pit of lions. Order this to be written and then sign it, so it can't be changed, just as no written law of the Medes and Persians can be changed." So King Darius made the law and had it written down. Daniel heard about the law, but when he returned home, he went upstairs and prayed in front of the window that faced Jerusalem. In the same way that he had always done, he knelt down in prayer three times a day, giving thanks to God.

Daniel 6:6-10

Newsflash: WILL DANIEL DARE DEFY DARIUS?

What a decision for Daniel to make! Until now, Daniel had been able to serve both God and the king. Now prayer was illegal. Who would he put first?

 Help us to get into the habit of talking to you Lord, so when the pressure comes, we're ready for it.

The pit of lions

Daniel saved

The men then told the king, "That Jew named Daniel, who was brought here as a captive, refuses to obey you or the law that you ordered to be written. And he still prays to his god three times a day." The king was really upset to hear about this, and for the rest of the day he tried to think how he could save Daniel. At sunset ... Darius ordered Daniel to be brought out and thrown into a pit of lions. But he said to Daniel, "You have been faithful to your God, and I pray that he will rescue you."

Daniel 6:13-16

Newsflash: DANIEL DUMPED IN DEN – DESTINED TO BE DINNER!

The king knew that he had been outwitted by his jealous officials. But Daniel's prayerfulness and confidence impressed him so much that even he began to believe in Daniel's God, and prayed to him. Daniel knew he had to go on doing what God wanted, even if it got him into trouble. His life depended on God. Our lives do, too – all the time, even though we may not realise it.

Lord, we pray that, like Daniel's, our behaviour may help other people believe in God.

At daybreak the king got up and ran to the pit. He was anxious and shouted, "Daniel, you were faithful and served your God. Was he able to save you from the lions?" Daniel answered, "Your Majesty, my God knew that I was innocent, and he sent an angel to keep the lions from eating me ... The king was relieved to hear Daniel's voice, and he gave orders for him to be taken out of the pit. ... King Darius then sent this message to all people of every nation and race in the world: "Greetings to all of you! I command everyone in my kingdom to worship and honour the God of Daniel. He is the living God, the one who lives for ever."

Daniel 6:19-23, 25-26

Newsflash: DANIEL DEFIES DEATH – DARIUS DELIGHTED!

Who was more worried: Daniel, in the pit with a bunch of starving lions, or King Darius, breaking his own law by praying to Daniel's God? Sometimes God answers prayers just the way we've asked them. Sometimes he has something better for us. Daniel seemed to be ready for both.

Lord help us to trust and obey, like Daniel.

Bible heroes - Josiah

27

*K*ing at eight years old: what a responsibility! Even at that age, Josiah took his duties seriously. More importantly, he took God seriously. We can do the same, even when we're young. God is certainly very serious about us.

The story of Josiah shows him as a very wise king. He persevered in his search to know what God expected of him. Even when he discovered how sad God was that the people had been disobedient, Josiah kept trying. It was his perseverance with God that made him such a great king. He died while he was still quite a young man but he left behind people who had discovered God afresh. No wonder so much is written about Josiah in the Bible.

Josiah was eight years old when he became king of Judah, and he ruled for 31 years from Jerusalem ... Josiah always obeyed the Lord, just as his ancestor David had done. After Josiah had been king for 18 years, he told Shaphan, one of his highest officials: 'Go to the temple and ask Hilkiah the high priest to collect from the guards all the money that the people have donated .. (and) give it to the men supervising the repairs to the temple.'

2 Kings 22:1-5

When a new kid comes to your school how do you find out about them? What sort of questions do you ask them? 'Where do you live?' 'How old are you?' 'Do you have a dog?' 'What sports do you like?' These help you decide if you want the person to be your friend. Josiah knew that he liked God and wanted to be his friend. But he didn't yet know a lot about God. This week we'll see how Josiah went about getting to know God.

A five-word memory verse from our Bible passage is hidden below. Find it and remember it! *(Solution p. 95)*

N	K	F	S	Z	N	W	B	C
Z	E	E	B	N	M	R	E	X
R	H	A	I	S	O	J	L	C
T	T	K	L	H	M	Y	W	C
U	A	O	Y	W	L	H	A	Y
Q	R	I	N	S	A	O	B	Z
D	Q	J	O	B	E	Y	E	D
F	A	E	Y	D	M	O	S	X
D	D	U	Q	B	I	S	T	D

The book was found

 While Shaphan was at the temple, Hilkiah handed him a book and said, "Look what I found here in the temple – 'The Book of God's Law'." Shaphan read it, then went back to Josiah and reported, "Your officials collected the money in the temple and gave it to the men supervising the repairs. But there's something else, Your Majesty. The priest Hilkiah gave me this book". Then Shaphan read it out loud. When Josiah heard what was in 'The Book of God's Law', he tore his clothes in sorrow.

2 Kings 22:8-11

Can any of us remember trying to put a model car or plane together without the instructions? Josiah was trying to do what God wanted, but he knew that he needed to find out more about how to do this. When his secretary Shaphan found the special book of God's laws, Josiah realised that he and his people had to change the way they were living their lives. They had forgotten God's rules. They had been lost but now they were found. Where would you look to find information on how to live your life?

 Dear God, we want to please you, but we need help. Thank you for giving us the Bible to help us know you, and know how we should live our lives.

What will God do?

 Josiah called together five leading men. He said, "The Lord must be furious with me and everyone else in Judah, because our ancestors did not obey the laws written in this book. Go and find out what the Lord wants us to do." The five men left straight away and went to talk with Huldah the prophet ... when they met in her home, she said: "You were sent here by King Josiah, and this is what the Lord God of Israel says to him: "Josiah, I am the Lord! And I will see to it that this country and everyone living in it will be destroyed ... just as this book says."

2 Kings 22:12-16

Even when we have the instructions for making that model, we often have to ask someone older to help. Josiah was really determined to find out what God wanted. He asked all sorts of people to help him study the special law book. Who do we have who can help us understand the Bible?

 Thank you dear God for all the help you give us ... for the Bible, for parents, friends, Sunday school and Scripture teachers, youth group leaders, ministers and others. Help us to use their help well.

The Book was read

King Josiah called together the older leaders of Judah and Jerusalem. Then he went to the Lord's temple, together with the people. ... Finally, when everybody was there, he read aloud 'The Book of God's Law' that had been found in the temple. After Josiah had finished reading, he stood by one of the columns. He asked the people to promise in the Lord's name to faithfully obey the Lord and to follow his commands. The people agreed to do everything written in the book.

2 Kings 23:1-3

Josiah was so convinced of the importance of what the Book had to say that he brought his people together in the temple. Then he asked them to promise to keep God's laws and live as God wanted. Josiah knew that if they lived as people who followed God's ways, he would care for them as he had cared for Moses and Joshua.

Help us Lord, not just to read your instructions for living, not just to get help to understand them, but to make the extra effort to promise to keep on living as you want us to, not just for today, but this week, this month, this year and forever.

The Passover celebrated

Josiah told the people of Judah, "Celebrate Passover in honour of the Lord your God, just as it says in 'The Book of God's Law'." This festival had not been celebrated in this way since kings ruled Israel and Judah. But in Josiah's 18th year as king of Judah, everyone came to Jerusalem to celebrate Passover.

2 Kings 23:21-22 and 23

When something important happens, we often have a party to celebrate it. For some very important things, like birthdays and weddings, we celebrate them every year on the same date, just so we don't forget them. Hundreds of years before, the Jews had been miserable slaves in Egypt. God rescued them in an amazing way – remember the story of Moses? To remember what he had done, God told them to eat this special meal in a special way every year on the anniversary of their escape. But they and their children forgot. It's good to remember times when we know God has been very clearly at work in our lives. It helps us to keep our promise to follow him.

Thank you God for showing us in history how you help your people. Thank you that you help us today in every way.

5 Josiah tried hard

Josiah got rid of every disgusting person and thing in Judah and Jerusalem – including magicians, fortune-tellers, and idols. He did his best to obey every law written in the book that the priest Hilkiah found in the Lord's temple. No other king before or after Josiah tried as hard as he did to obey the Law of Moses.

2 Kings 23:24-25

Can you keep a secret? Have you ever been dying to tell somebody? Boy, can it be hard! Josiah kept his promises. They weren't secrets, but he had to work hard to keep them. He made a lot of changes in the way people lived. He closed down activities that God didn't like, and if people in important jobs weren't prepared to follow God, he fired them. The Bible says that 'he served the Lord with all his heart, mind and strength'. This sounds strangely like what Jesus said was the most important thing ever. Does anybody know what that was? Check out Mark 12:29-30.

Dear Lord, it's hard some-times to keep the promises we make to you, especially when other people around us are going the opposite way. But we want to please you. Help us to keep on keeping on, in front of our family and friends and others.

Memory verse solution from page 92.
'Josiah always obeyed the Lord.'

28

Good news

A holiday in winter

*H*olidays are a good opportunity to stop and think. When we get out of our regular routine, we can see things differently. Paul wrote a letter to the Christians in Colossae because they were beginning to get things wrong. They were forgetting Jesus comes first and that they needed to worship him. They needed to get back to basics and see things clearly again. Holidays in winter can be a time when we spend less time out of doors and more time inside. That gives us more time to do things together and to spend time thinking about Jesus.

Good news

  ## Wonderful kingdom

Each time we pray for you, we thank God, the Father of our Lord Jesus Christ. We have heard of your faith in Christ and of your love for all of God's people, because what you hope for is kept safe for you in heaven. You first heard about this hope when you believed the true message, which is the good news.

Colossians 1:3-5

The good news is spreading all over the world with great success. It has spread in that same way among you, ever since the first day you learned the truth about God's wonderful kindness from our good friend Epaphras. He works together with us for Christ and is a faithful worker for you. He is also the one who told us about the love that God's spirit has given you.

Colossians 1:6-8

Paul prayed a lot for the many churches he visited or contacted. Paul knew that the Christians in Colossae knew the good news. They knew about Jesus. They knew that he died and rose again. They put their trust and their hope in Jesus. The good news was spreading all over the world. What are some of the places we know where the good news is being shared today? What missionaries have told us about their work? Who has read something about sharing the good news in a magazine? Who can name countries where the good news is being spread? Can we look them up on a map of the world? See how far they are away and how big they are. Pray for the people in these countries and those who are sharing the good news.

God is wonderfully kind to us. We really don't deserve it. After all, we do so many wrong things that make him very sad. He understands – that's why Jesus came, so that we could believe in him and trust him to forgive us. When Jesus died on the cross, he took the wrong doing of the whole world on himself. It was as if he were punished for every wrong that every person ever did. That was wonderful kindness. All God wants is that we ask Jesus to be our friend by saying sorry and promising to follow him. That's what the good news is all about. The Christians in Colossae knew that because Epaphras had told them. Now Epaphras and Paul were in prison but they still rejoiced because of God's wonderful kindness.

 Dear Lord Jesus, thank you that I can be forgiven for all the wrong things I do by saying sorry and meaning it. Thank you for loving me so much.

2 Don't stop praying

3 God rescued us

We have not stopped praying for you since the first day we heard about you. In fact, we always pray that God will show you everything he wants you to do and that you may have all the wisdom and understanding that his Spirit gives. Then you will live a life that honours the Lord, and you will always please him by doing good deeds. You will come to know God even better. His glorious power will make you patient and strong enough to endure anything and you will be truly happy.

Colossians 1:9-11

Paul doesn't stop with the good news about Jesus. He goes on praying for the Christians in Colossae. He wants those Christians to show they love God by being wise and doing good deeds. Paul knew that churches would grow when Christians loved one another. The sort of love Paul was thinking about was very practical. It was about helping each other and putting other people first. Paul knew they might be punished for being Christians just like he was. They needed to be strong so that they could put up with being in trouble. He knew that whatever happened they would be truly happy if they loved and trusted Jesus.

Thank you Lord Jesus that people pray for us. Help us to be wise and do good things for other people.

I pray that you will be grateful to God for letting you have part in what he has promised his people in the kingdom of light. God rescued us from the dark power of Satan and brought us into the kingdom of his dear Son, who forgives our sins and sets us free.

Colossians 1:12-14

God is light. Where God is, everything can be seen and understood. Nothing can be hidden from God. Sometimes when we have done something wrong, we want to hide so that no one can see us. God doesn't want us to be like that – he rescued us from hiding in the dark. Paul says Jesus forgives our sins and sets us free. When we are free, we need not be ashamed. Paul wants these Christians to be like Jesus so that they can be free. Paul reminds them that following Jesus is like being where it is always light and where no one needs to hide. Do you feel like hiding sometimes? Remember Jesus wants to save you from hiding and help you to be more like him.

Dear Lord Jesus, thank you for rescuing me and setting me free. Help me to please you by what I do.

Jesus the Lord

*Christ is exactly like God, who
    cannot be seen.
He is the firstborn Son, superior to
    all creation.
Everything was created by him,
everything in heaven and on
    earth,
everything seen and unseen,
including all forces and powers,
and all rulers and authorities.
All things were created by
    God's Son
and everything was made for him.*

*God's Son was before all else,
and by him everything is held
    together.
He is the head of his body which
    is the church.
He is the very beginning,
the first to be raised from death,
so that he would be above all
    others.*

Colossians 1:15-18

This is a very old hymn about Jesus.
What do you learn about Jesus from it?
Are there things you don't understand?
You might know a modern song about
Jesus that you could sing and compare
it with this old song. Simply, it tells us
how wonderful Jesus is. He is the one
who is above everything else. Jesus,
this wonderful king, wants to be your
friend.

Lord Jesus, you are above all
others. Help us to worship you
and love you today.

 # Peace with the Lord

*God himself was pleased to live
fully in his Son. And God was
pleased for him to make peace by
sacrificing his blood on the cross,
so that all beings in heaven and
on earth would be brought back
to God.*

*You used to be far from God. Your
thoughts made you his enemies,
and you did evil things. But his
Son became a human and died.
So God made peace with you,
and now he lets you stand in his
presence as people who are holy
and faultless and innocent.*

Colossians 1:19-22

What a wonderful promise! Because of
Jesus we can come to God and tell him
everything. We need not be afraid
because God has made peace with us.
That means we can be his friend and
he will love us and care for us. Sometimes we do feel as if we are a long
way away from God. That may be what
we feel but it isn't true. God is always
near. God is always waiting to listen
to us. We need not be afraid of him
because God chose to make peace with
us, to love us. There was nothing we
could do because we were far away.
God did everything so all we need to
do is thank him, trust him and follow
him.

Thank you Heavenly Father
for loving us so much that we
need never be afraid again.
Thank you for giving us peace
that comes through Jesus.

Stories Jesus told 2

J esus told many stories. Some of them were about the Kingdom of Heaven. The Kingdom of Heaven is where God rules. John the Baptist announced that the Kingdom was present and he pointed to Jesus. When Jesus was alive, he showed people that the Kingdom was present by healing people and casting out demons. God's kingdom is present in the world today but like the mustard seed, it isn't always seen. One day, God's kingdom will be recognised by everybody. At the moment we have to wait. We look out for where God is at work and he is especially at work calling people to follow him as a friend of Jesus.

 Jesus asked his disciples if they understood all these things. They said, "Yes we do." So he told them, "Every student of the Scriptures who becomes a disciple in the kingdom of heaven is like someone who brings out new and old treasures from the storeroom." When Jesus had finished telling these stories, he left and went to his home town. He taught in their meeting place and the people were so amazed that they asked, "Where does he get all this wisdom and the power to work these miracles?"

Matthew 13:51-54

Do you enjoy watching a magician do his tricks? It's amazing what they can do? It must take a lot of practice and patience. Who can do magic tricks? Jesus had just told some parables. He asked his disciples if they had understood them. What was their answer? Jesus went on to say that his followers who read the Bible will learn new things and be reminded of what they already know. What do you already know about Jesus? Jesus then went to his home town of Nazareth. He taught the people about God and did some miracles. The people were amazed that he knew so much and did such wonderful miracles. 'How can he do all this?' they said. Jesus wasn't a magician. How did he have such power and wisdom?

The lost sheep

 "Let me ask you this. 'What would you do if you had 100 sheep and one of them wandered off? Wouldn't you leave the 99 on the hillside to go and look for the one that had wandered off? I am sure that finding it would make you happier than having the 99 that never wandered off. That's how it is with your Father in heaven. He doesn't want any of these little ones to be lost."

Matthew 18:12-14

How do you feel when you can't find something precious to you? It may be a pet, your basketball cap, a toy you take to bed, your diary, car keys or glasses! We may have other caps, toys, keys, pets or glasses but it just isn't the same as the missing one. How do you feel when it's found? Jesus told a parable to show how much he cares for each person in his family. He doesn't want anyone to miss out on the good things he has for them. The story is about someone who has 100 sheep but one gets lost. The person leaves the 99 safe sheep to look for the missing one. How did he feel when he found the lost sheep? The lost one becomes very precious.

 Thank you Jesus, that you love and care for us. Thank you that you don't want us to miss out on the good things you have for us.

The mustard seed

 Jesus told them another story: "The kingdom of heaven is like what happens when a farmer plants a mustard seed in a field. Although it's the smallest of all seeds, it grows larger than any garden plant and becomes a tree. Birds even come and nest in its branches."

Matthew 13:31-32

When Olympic athletes win gold medals they become famous heroes. Most of them have never been heard of until they become a gold medallist. This great achievement probably started for them when they were young. Perhaps they did well in a school competition. Their small beginnings took a lot of training and perseverance to turn them into world champions. This parable is about God's kingdom. God's kingdom is wherever God is king. Wherever God is king, his love will be found. Jesus said God's kingdom is like a mustard seed. It is one of the smallest seeds in the world. But it grows and grows and grows! When it is fully grown it is one of the biggest trees. God's kingdom can start very small. God's love may only be in one person's heart, but when his love is shared, his kingdom grows and grows. How can you help spread God's love?

 Dear God, thank you for your love. Help us to share your love with others and make your kingdom bigger.

3 The good seed

 Then he taught them many things by using stories. He said: "A farmer went out to scatter seed in a field. While the farmer was scattering the seed, some of it fell along the road and was eaten by birds. Other seeds fell on thin, rocky ground and quickly started growing because the soil wasn't very deep. But when the sun came up, the plants were scorched and dried up, because they didn't have enough roots. Some other seeds fell where thorn bushes grew up and choked the plants. But a few seeds did fall on good ground where the plants produced 100 or 60 or 30 times as much as was scattered."

Matthew 13:3-8

What do seeds need to grow into strong, healthy plants? Good soil, sunshine, water and no weeds. Where did this seed fall and what happened? The seed is the news about God. The birds, thorn bushes and rocks are like some people's hearts. They hear God's word but they have their hearts on other things. They do not love God and don't follow him. The good ground is like the hearts of people who understand. They love God. God's love grows in their hearts like a beautiful, healthy plant.

 Heavenly Father, thank you for the people we know who love God. Be with them today.

4 The hidden treasure

 The kingdom of heaven is like what happens when someone finds treasure hidden in a field and buries it again. A person like that is happy and goes and sells everything in order to buy that field. The kingdom of heaven is like what happens when a shop owner is looking for fine pearls. After finding a very valuable one, the owner goes and sells everything in order to buy that pearl.

Matthew 13:44-46

Have you ever been given an unexpected present when it wasn't your birthday or Christmas? 'God's kingdom is like a treasure,' said Jesus. It is like a treasure hidden in a field. A man was working in the field. He did not know about the treasure. Tap. Tap. His shovel bumped something. He looked at it and dusted it off. It was real treasure! He was so excited! He quickly hid the treasure again. Then he sold everything he had. He took the money and bought the field. Then he ran back and dug up the treasure. What had he given up to get the treasure? How did he feel? Jesus also said the kingdom of heaven is like a valuable pearl. God's kingdom is perfect like the pearl. It is better than anything else in the world. It is worth anything you might give up for it.

 Thank you God that we belong to your kingdom. Help us to learn what it means to have you as our king.

The two sons

Jesus said: "I'll tell you a story about a man who had two sons. Then you can tell me what you think. The father went to the older son and said 'Go and work in the vineyard today!' His son told him that he wouldn't do it, but later he changed his mind and went. The man then told his younger son to go and work in the vineyard. The boy said he would , but he didn't go. Which one of the sons obeyed the father?" "The older one," the chief priests and leaders answered. Then Jesus told them, "You can be sure that tax collectors and prostitutes will get into the kingdom of God before you ever will!"

Matthew 21: 28-31

There's a saying 'actions speak louder than words.' Jesus is in the temple church talking with the teachers of the Old Testament and some leaders. They questioned Jesus about what he had been doing and who gave him permission. Which son's actions spoke louder than his words? The older son stands for the people that weren't liked in Jesus' time. The younger son is like the leaders and teachers. They knew all the right things to say but didn't do them. Jesus is more interested in what we do than what we say.

Lord Jesus, we are sorry when we don't do the right thing. Help us to do the things that please you.

Merry-go-round the Bible

A dangerous time

Winter

In many places, winter is a time of great relief from summer heat and storms. For other people, winter is a time of snow and frost and cold. The book called Acts was written in the northern hemisphere. It was quite dangerous to travel in winter when strong winds could blow ships off course and onto rocks. The story we are reading this week is about a storm and shipwreck. Paul warned the ship captain not to sail because God had told him they would be wrecked. But the ship sailed and disaster struck. However, God still had a job for Paul to do, so Paul and all the other people on the boat were rescued. God is in control even when everything seems to go wrong.

W.E. Winter

1. A strong mind

By now we had already lost a lot of time, and sailing was no longer safe. In fact, even the Great Day of Forgiveness was past. Then Paul spoke to the crew of the ship, "Men listen to me! If we sail now, our ship and its cargo will be badly damaged and many lives will be lost." But Julius listened to the captain of the ship and its owner, rather than to Paul. The harbour at Fair Havens wasn't a good place to spend the winter. Because of this, almost everyone agreed that we should at least try and to sail along the coast of Crete as far as Phoenix. It had a harbour that opened towards the south-west and north-west and we could spend the winter there.

Acts 27:9-12

The weather affects many things we do. Should we play outside or inside or do the gardening or tidy the bedroom? Lots of things depend on the weather. Paul was on his way to Rome. He had been arrested and was being escorted by a Roman soldier called Julius. Paul trusted in God. Because he loved God he was concerned for the safety of everyone else on the boat. The ship's captain ignored Paul's advice and set sail. Think of things we have planned because we listened to the weather forecast? What have we decided to do this weekend because of the weather? Let's make a weather chart for the week and each day write down what the weather was like and what we did because it was that sort of weather. Thank God that some days are sunny and some are wet.

When a gentle wind from the south started blowing, the men thought it was a good time to do what they had planned. So they pulled up the anchor and we sailed along the coast of Crete. But soon a strong wind called the 'North-easter' blew against us from the island. The wind struck the ship and we couldn't sail against it. So we let the wind carry the ship.

Act 27:13-15

There's an old saying 'The best laid plans of mice and men often go wrong.' The ship set sail in a gentle wind but soon a very strong wind came. Has that happened to us? It doesn't look like rain so we do something outdoors, then it suddenly pours down. The sailors let the wind blow the ship along. They didn't know where they were going. They began to get frightened. It is easy to be frightened when things go wrong and we don't know what to do. Can you remember that happening to you? But one person in the ship remained calm – that was Paul. Paul knew that God was in control. Paul was happy to trust God even as the winds blew stronger and stronger.

Dear Lord Jesus, help me to remain calm when things go wrong. Help me to trust in you. You love me and will care for me.

103

2 A fierce storm

The storm was so fierce that the next day they threw some of the ship's cargo overboard. Then on the third day, with their bare hands they threw overboard some of the ship's gear. For several days we couldn't see either the sun or the stars. A strong wind kept blowing and we finally gave up all hope of being saved. Since none of us had eaten anything for a long time, Paul stood up and told the men, "You should have listened to me! If you had stayed on in Crete, you wouldn't have had this damage and loss. But now I beg you to cheer up, because you will be safe. Only the ship will be lost."

Acts 27:18-22

Things went from bad to worse. With no sun or stars visible the ship's crew had no idea where they were. The heavily laden ship was in trouble. They threw out the cargo and all the extras on the ship, trying to save themselves from sinking. Only Paul stayed calm. He reminded them that they should never have set out on the journey. But as they had done so, the ship would be lost. Everyone on board would be safe. Probably people thought Paul was mad. How could he be so confident that they would be safe? With the wind howling and the sea roaring it didn't look very hopeful. Paul went on trusting God.

Heavenly Father, help us to trust you when things go wrong.

3 God's promise

"I belong to God and I worship him. Last night he sent an angel to tell me, 'Paul don't be afraid! You will stand trial before the emperor. And because of you, God will save the lives of everyone on the ship.' Cheer up! I am sure that God will do exactly what he promised. But we will first be shipwrecked on some island."

Acts 27:23-26

What an amazing message! The angel told Paul not to be afraid because God had something for him to do. God wanted him to tell the Roman emperor and all his court about Jesus. Paul told the people on the ship they would be safe. That was a great message. Probably some of the travellers believed Paul but many would think him mad. They didn't know anything about this God Paul talked about. Who was he? Paul didn't have a statue of him or a picture. He couldn't be real. Would you have believed Paul? Paul persisted, he trusted God to keep his word even when people didn't believe what he said.

Lord Jesus, it is hard sometimes to believe your promises. Give us the faith today to trust you and follow you.

4 Be encouraged!

 Just before daylight, Paul begged the people to eat something. He told them, "For 14 days you've been so worried that you haven't eaten a thing. I beg you to eat something. Your lives depend on it. Do this and not one of you will be hurt." After Paul had said this, he took a piece of bread and gave thanks to God. Then in front of everyone he broke the bread and ate some. They all felt encouraged and each of them ate something.

Acts 27:33-36

Paul sensed that everyone was weak. They had not eaten for 14 days but needed strength to survive the shipwreck. What did Paul do? Paul began to eat food after he had thanked God. Paul not only told them what to do, he encouraged them and ate himself. God often wants us to encourage each other. Sometimes he wants us to do something to show we mean what we say. Everyone felt better when they had eaten. Paul's example helped them. Not only did he stay calm but he took practical steps to make sure they were ready when the ship struck the rock.

 Lord Jesus, help us to encourage each other today whatever the problems. Help us to do things that will show others we really care about them.

 # 5 Everyone safe

 They raised the sail at the front of the ship and let the wind carry the ship towards the beach. But it ran aground on a sandbank. The front of the ship stuck firmly in the sand and the rudder was smashed by the force of the waves. The soldiers decided to kill the prisoners to keep them from swimming away and escaping. But Captain Julius wanted to save Paul's life, and he didn't let the soldiers do what they had planned. Instead, he ordered everyone who could swim to dive into the water and head for shore. Then he told the others to hold on to planks of wood or parts of the ship. At last, everyone safely reached shore.

Acts 27:40-44

Stuck on a sandbank, pounded by waves, the ship began to break up. The Roman soldiers knew that if their prisoners escaped they were liable to take their punishment. If the prisoners were killed, they couldn't run away. Julius had different ideas. Despite big waves and fierce winds everyone got to shore. That was God's promise and he always keeps his word. The sailors would have told the story over and over again. Perhaps they remembered that Paul had said God would save them all.

 Thank you Lord, that we can trust you to keep your promises. Help us to remember that you really love us and care about us.

Where to find Scripture Union

Australia
PO Box 2915, Fitzroy DC, Victoria 3065

Canada
1885 Clements Road, Unit 226, Pickering, Ontario LIW 3V4

England & Wales
207-209 Queensway, Bletchley, Milton Keynes,
Bucks MK2 3EB, England

Fiji
PO Box 1278, Suva

New Zealand
PO Box 760, Wellington

Northern Ireland
157 Albertbridge Road, Belfast BT5 4PS

Papua New Guinea
PO Box 280, University, NCD

Peninsular Malaysia
386 Jalan 5/59, 46000 Petaling Jaya, Selangor

Scotland
9 Canal Street, Glasgow G4 OAB

Singapore
#03-07, 7 Armenian Street, Singapore 179932

Solomon Islands
PO Box 294, Honiara

South Africa
PO Box 291, Rondebosch 7700, Cape Town

Tonga
PO Box 825, Nuku'alofa

USA
Suite 215, 150 Strafford Avenue, Wayne, PA 19087

Vanuatu
PO Box 379, Port Vila

International Office
59 Princess Road West, Leicester LEI 6TR, England